MW01491993

BUILDING
Momentum

GARY NICHOLSON

LifeWay Press®
Nashville, Tennessee

ISBN 978-1-4158-6883-6 • Item 005271229

Dewey decimal classification: 726
Subject headings: CHURCH ARCHITECTURE \ CHURCH BUILDINGS

Unless otherwise noted, all Scripture quotations are taken from the Holman Christian Standard Bible®, copyright © 1999, 2000, 2001, 2002, 2003 by Holman Bible Publishers. Used by permission.

To order additional copies of this resource, write to LifeWay Church Resources Customer Service; One LifeWay Plaza; Nashville, TN 37234-0113; fax (615) 251-5933; order online at *www.lifeway.com;* phone toll free (800) 458-2772; e-mail *orderentry@lifeway.com;* or visit the LifeWay Christian Store serving you.

Printed in Canada

Leadership and Adult Publishing; LifeWay Church Resources; One LifeWay Plaza; Nashville, TN 37234-0175

CONTENTS

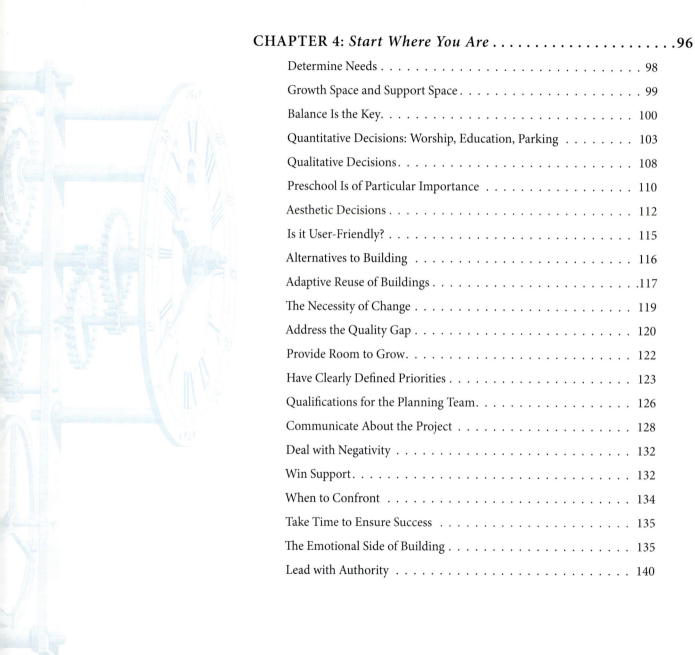

THE AUTHOR

GARY NICHOLSON has served as the director of LifeWay Architecture since 2006. He has a bachelor of architecture from the University of Texas at Austin and a master of divinity from New Orleans Baptist Theological Seminary. He is a licensed Southern Baptist minister who has more than 10 years of experience on church staffs. Since coming to LifeWay in 1993, Gary has helped hundreds of churches make wise decisions about their building projects, from deciding what to build to compiling the final punch list.

With a passion for the Great Commission, Gary has contributed numerous articles to periodicals and has led many seminars and conferences, addressing church leaders and architects who work with churches. He has successfully designed hundreds of churches across the United States, from small, first-unit buildings to hundred-acre megachurch campuses. His 34 years of varied experience have earned him great respect for his valuable insight and advice for leaders of any size church. Gary is a member of the American Institute of Architects, a national professional organization for architects.

DEDICATION

This book is dedicated to the staff
of LifeWay Architecture.

LifeWay Architecture is a team of talented and wise people who have done excellent work for many years to help churches through the process of building. Although the department has existed since 1917, there was a major resurgence in this area in the mid 1990s, and from that time forward, it has become a more professional and beneficial resource to churches. I want to thank two former directors, Gwenn McCormick and Davis Byrd, for bringing me to the department and nurturing me along the way.

I especially want to acknowledge the contribution of Steve Newton to the ideas in this book. His views on master planning and church growth are represented throughout this book. Steve and I worked together to create an entirely new approach to church master planning that guides much of the work our department does with churches and the advice that is given in this book. No one in the world is better than Steve at discerning and guiding churches to do the right thing.

I want to thank my family   Amy; Paul; Christy, and my wife, Kaye—for their patience as I traveled around the country from church to church for the past 17 years consulting with churches and learning the truths that are contained in this book. They have always been a huge part of my ministry with churches, and I could not have done it without their love, support, encouragement, and patience. I love you!

I want to thank the many churches that I have had the privilege to work with over these years. God bless them and their desire to fulfill the Great Commission. A lot of good church leaders are out there, and I thank God for each of you.

Finally, this book is dedicated to the memory of my father, Ed Nicholson, a dedicated and talented architect who taught me more than I can say about architecture. Dad passed away a few months ago, and I will miss him; but part of him lives in me and in every design that comes out of my pencil.

INTRODUCTION

Your Role as a Leader

Building Momentum is about moving the church toward a goal.

The goal is not just to construct a new building but to equip the church for the important work of the kingdom of God. Church leaders are responsible for placing the church in the best possible position to fulfill the Great Commission and to ensure success. To achieve the greatest potential for the project, the leadership team needs to set the pace of the project to constantly move it in a positive direction, building momentum throughout the process. Eventually, the entire process climaxes with a celebration at the opening of the new facility with all church programs and leaders in place, ready to launch a new era in the life of the church.

YOU ARE A LEADER. Whether you are the pastor, a member of the leadership team, a staff member, a deacon, or the chair of the project team, you are in a position of leadership. Someone has seen in you the qualities of a leader who can help guide the church through a building project. People will look to you to show them how to react and behave in regard to your project. If you are a good leader, they will see you model behavior that is healthy for the church. If not, as you are probably keenly aware, you could inadvertently lead them in the wrong direction. One quality of a good leader is that he or she can get things done. Mediocre or poor leaders take too long or never quite seem to be able to get it done.

People will take their cues from you to either support or reject a proposed project. They respect you. That is why you are in this position. The segment of the congregation you influence may be large or small; that does not matter. It is your responsibility to be sure your influence is what it should be so that you can lead them in the right direction. You no longer have the luxury of kibitzing from the sidelines; you are in the game now. This is your project, your responsibility.

BUILDING A CHURCH FACILITY IS A SPIRITUAL TASK. It is not like any other building project. Anyone who tells you otherwise doesn't understand what is at stake. This time is a key time in the life of the church. Buildings take up enormous amounts of time, money, and human resources. To succeed is to launch the church forward into a new set of capabilities. To fail can hinder the church from accomplishing its purpose of reaching people for Christ and/or burden the church with all kinds of problems.

Projects that go wrong generally fall into one of four categories: wrong timing, financing errors, design problems, or a breakdown in relationships. Sometimes these combine to sabotage the intended purpose of the project, but any one of these issues can be enough to create significant problems before, during, or after the project.

A building project must be done at the right time in the life of the church in order to coincide with the window of opportunity that God intends for the church. A project should not leave the church in debt, burdened with payments that strangle its ability to do ministry. A church that does a good job of discovering its real needs will find that it has met the critical needs of the ministry. Some churches find that the most difficult part of the process of building is maintaining the relational fabric of the congregation. Factions may develop and must be addressed. A common sense of purpose should keep the people together and the project on target. The leaders' goal is to see the project through on time, on budget, and with the right design that meets the needs of the church while maintaining the congregation's common focus on the mission of the church.

It can be done! In fact, it is not as hard as it may seem. But success will take a team of leaders in the church, working with quality professionals from outside the church, to combine their talents, keep their focus, and remain sensitive to the calling of God.

> **BEWARE** *of the* **FOUR DANGERS**
>
> 1. Bad timing
> 2. Financing errors
> 3. Design problems
> 4. Relationship breakdowns

CHAPTER 1

Lay the Spiritual Foundation

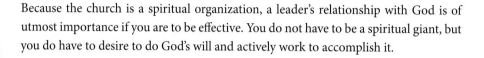

Good leadership starts and ends
with your relationship with God.

Because the church is a spiritual organization, a leader's relationship with God is of utmost importance if you are to be effective. You do not have to be a spiritual giant, but you do have to desire to do God's will and actively work to accomplish it.

Seven Roles of a Spiritual Leader

A leader in the position of planning and building a church facility must fulfill at least seven roles.

1. Visionary. As with any journey, you must start with the destination in mind. If you don't know where you are going, as the Cheshire cat in *Alice in Wonderland* said, "then it doesn't matter which way you go." A spiritual leader gets his or her direction from an intimate relationship with God. "Trust in the Lord with all your heart, and do not rely on your own understanding; think about Him in all your ways, and He will guide you on the right paths" (Prov. 3:5-6).

2. Strategist. As a leader, you must be prepared to think through a history of past events, to understand the current state and current needs, and to see the possibilities for the future. Then you must map a strategy of appropriate actions to get your church from where it is today to where God wants you to make a positive impact on that community for Christ. "I will lead the blind by a way they did not know; I will guide them on paths they have not known. I will turn darkness to light in front of them, and rough places into level ground" (Isa. 42:16).

3. MARKETING EXPERT. Your understanding of the culture of your church, its strengths, and the community you serve puts you in the best position to communicate both to the rest of the congregation and to the community at large. Knowing the right thing to do and how to do it will amount to nothing if you cannot persuade others of their merits. Work at getting the point across so that everyone can grasp the ideas and see why the action is appropriate, necessary, and desirable. Let God speak through you as He did the prophet Jeremiah: "The LORD said to me: Do not say: I am only a youth, for you will go to everyone I send you to and speak whatever I tell you. Do not be afraid of anyone, for I will be with you to deliver you. This is the LORD's declaration. Then the LORD reached out His hand, touched my mouth, and told me: Look, I have filled your mouth with My words. See, today I have set you over nations and kingdoms to uproot and tear down, to destroy and demolish, to build and plant" (Jer. 1:7-10).

4. STUDENT. If you think you have all the answers, you probably don't understand the question! Being teachable is important to growth, and growth is what being a Christian leader is really all about. You need to be willing to learn from Scripture and learn from others, both young and old, and inspire others to do the same. Answers can come from some of the most surprising places. Listen with new ears to those around you, and you might find that God has provided more wisdom than you ever dreamed. "It was good for me to be afflicted so that I could learn Your statutes. Instruction from Your lips is better for me than thousands of gold and silver pieces" (Ps. 119:71-72).

5. INVENTOR. You need to spearhead the development of new ideas and approaches to meet the needs that are discovered. Creative solutions can allow the church to do more with less. Design programs to make the most of the resources you have. Plan facilities to meet multiple needs rather than using a conventional approach to ministry and facilities that can be wasteful and expensive. "Look, I am about to do something new; even now it is coming. Do you not see it? Indeed, I will make a way in the wilderness, rivers in the desert" (Isa. 43:19).

SEVEN ROLES *of a* SPIRITUAL LEADER

1. Visionary
2. Strategist
3. Marketing expert
4. Student
5. Inventor
6. Coach
7. Role model

6. COACH. To be the kind of leader found in the New Testament, you will need to pass on what you learn to others. Aiding the growth of others is as much a part of your job description as anything else. "What you have heard from me in the presence of many witnesses, commit to faithful men who will be able to teach others also" (2 Tim. 2:2).

7. ROLE MODEL. There is no substitute for a good role model for others to see and emulate. Our ultimate role model is Christ Himself, but many people need to see self-less love and the Christian life offered as a living sacrifice in the flesh day by day to understand how to live. They need to see you lean on Jesus and point to Him as your example in everything. "Brothers, by the mercies of God, I urge you to present your bodies as a living sacrifice, holy and pleasing to God; this is your spiritual worship. Do not be conformed to this age, but be transformed by the renewing of your mind, so that you may discern what is the good, pleasing, and perfect will of God" (Rom. 12:1-2).

Learning from Nehemiah

We can learn a lot from Nehemiah. God called him to go and rebuild the walls of Jerusalem after he and his fellow Israelites had been in captivity in Babylon for more than 70 years. As he took on this task, he encountered many of the same challenges we confront in church projects today.

THE VISION

Nehemiah was living in exile as a servant to King Artaxerxes in the city of Susa, miles away from the country he loved. He did not hold a position in the Jewish religious hier-archy. He was not a Levite, a priest, a temple servant, a scribe, or a prophet. He was just an ordinary man with a desire to obey God. He had a passion for correcting a situation that needed to be corrected. Hanani, Nehemiah's brother, had just come from Judah, their homeland. When he saw him, Nehemiah asked about the conditions back home. The news was not good. The walls of Jerusalem were in ruins.

The news stirred something in Nehemiah that made him want to act. Sad, he sat down and wept and mourned, but he did not stop there. He set out to do something about it.

You may discover your church's need to build in a number of ways. Someone may have done a study, or it may have come up in conversation. You may not even be sure the need really exists. Whether the need is real will soon become apparent once the proper preparation is done. Your job at this point is to do as Nehemiah did and make yourself available to God as He works His plan.

Nehemiah prayed, acknowledging that the nation of Israel had sinned and brought disaster on themselves through their disobedience. He remembered that their circumstance fulfilled a promise God had given Moses: "If you are unfaithful, I will scatter you among the peoples" (Neh. 1:8). But as Nehemiah prayed, he remembered another promise God had given Moses: "If you return to Me and carefully observe My commands, even though your exiles were banished to the ends of the earth, I will gather them from there and bring them to the place where I chose to have My name dwell" (Neh. 1:9).

This was a prayer of commitment. Nehemiah said he was ready to lead his fellow Israelites to be obedient: "They are Your servants and Your people. You redeemed them by Your great power and strong hand. Please, Lord, let Your ear be attentive to the prayer of Your servant and to that of Your servants who delight to revere Your name" (Neh. 1:10-11). Notice that Nehemiah did not tell God they were going to be obedient, but he asked God to observe whether they demonstrated their obedience. Actions are all that really count. As one preacher used to say, "What we do is what we believe; the rest is just religious talk."

Nehemiah ended his prayer with a simple, straightforward request, "Give Your servant success today, and have compassion on him in the presence of this man" (Neh. 1:11). Nehemiah had a plan. He would ask the king for permission to restore the walls of the city. He planned to do the legwork, but he knew it was God who could bring success.

Nehemiah had a plan. He planned to do the legwork, but he knew it was God who could bring success.

BEFORE THE KING

Nehemiah never even had to bring up the subject. Seeing that he was sad, the king asked Nehemiah what was on his mind. Because it was a crime punishable by death to be sad in the presence of the king, Nehemiah was running a great risk by letting his countenance reveal what was on his heart. But because part of his responsibility as the king's cupbearer was to taste the king's food for poison, he had earned the king's trust.

Although Nehemiah was "overwhelmed with fear" (Neh. 2:2), he explained the situation and made his request. The king asked how long it would take, and with his answer Nehemiah had permission to go. Just like that! He didn't let his fear stop him. He was a brave man. Courage is a mark of a great leader.

At the beginning of your church's project, your prayer should be like Nehemiah's, first committing yourself to God to be obedient. You cannot commit for anyone but yourself. However, you can promise to encourage others to be obedient by your example of obedience and by your verbal testimony. Earnestly commit to God to do what needs to be done for the good of His kingdom, regardless of the personal price to be paid.

OPPOSITION ARISES

Nehemiah began by quietly planning the project, arriving on site, and presenting his letters from the king to the governors of the region. Immediately, he began to encounter opposition. In Nehemiah 2:10 we see that "when Sanballat the Horonite and Tobiah the Ammonite official heard that someone had come to seek the well-being of the Israelites, they were greatly displeased." We don't know how they found out, but Nehemiah had not even told his own men what he had planned.

You will encounter opposition in whatever project you decide to take on. It may be from inside or outside the church or both. You can count on it! Sometimes the opposition comes from a source from which you least expect it. Other times it is very predictable.

PLANNING BEGINS

Nehemiah began to plan the building project by personally inspecting the rubble of the old wall, out of the view of the public, in order to understand the situation and what he would be asking his people to do. His next move was to honestly describe the situation to the people who could do something about it. He pointed out that the city and its walls were completely in ruins and the city was defenseless. He described the way God had called him and what the king had told him. Then he told them the nature of the project and his motive: "Come, let's rebuild Jerusalem's wall, so that we will no longer be a disgrace" (Neh. 2:17).

The response was positive. The people said, "Let's start rebuilding!"

If you are honest with your people and help them not only see the task but also understand the calling and the reason behind it, you begin to cast a vision. By sharing the existing situation, the desired outcome, and the means to get there, a leader can give the people the right combination of information and inspiration to get behind the project and enthusiastically join the effort.

A leader can give the people the right combination of information and inspiration to get behind the project and enthusiastically join the effort.

THE OPPOSITION'S FIRST ATTACK

As you may soon learn, word travels fast on a project like this, and when Sanballat, Tobiah, and Geshem heard about it, they "mocked and despised" them, asking, "Are you rebelling against the king?" (Neh. 2:19). When an enemy attacks with words, it stings the most when those words have an element of truth. The Israelites would have loved to be powerful enough to rebel and gain their freedom, but they knew they had no chance against the powerful forces of King Artaxerxes. This is why the words of Sanballat and friends hurt.

Many times words of discouragement come from your own heart. You are unsure of your abilities. These thoughts haunt you, asking, *What if you fail? Are you up to leading a church into a massive building project? Do you even know what you are doing?*

Nehemiah responded to his critics by saying, "The God of heaven is the One who will grant us success. We, His servants, will start building, but you have no share, right, or historic claim in Jerusalem" (Neh. 2:20). Note several things about his response.

NEHEMIAH WAS GOD-CENTERED. God is the one who calls you, and He will give you success. Your abilities are not being tested. God's are, and He is faithful!

NEHEMIAH WAS CONFIDENT. Faith speaks with confidence but not beyond what God has revealed to us. He doesn't say we will try to make it happen, but we will start building. Notice he didn't say we will finish. He wasn't presuming God would let them finish. It was as if he were saying, "All I know is that God told us to start. That's what we will do, and He will determine what happens after that."

NEHEMIAH WAS DIRECT. He let his enemies know they were out of line and in for some stiff competition if they were going to tangle with him. You must take this job seriously and not let anyone get in the way of doing what God has called you to do.

THE WORK BEGINS

Nehemiah set the workers to the task. In Nehemiah 3 we see the workers side by side: the goldsmith, the perfumer, the rulers, the Levites, the merchants, the priests, and the temple servants worked right alongside the rest of the people. When their self-proclaimed enemy, Sanballat, heard that the work had started, he was furious. This time he mocked the Jews, publicly calling them "pathetic Jews" (Neh. 4:2). His fellow troublemaker, Tobiah, joined in with sarcasm: "If a fox climbed up what they are building, he would break down their stone wall!" (Neh. 4:3).

Once again their attack was on target. These were not professional stonemasons and gate builders. This kind of work was not at all in their comfort zones. You might feel a little out of your comfort zone too. Even if you've built a house before or even a commercial building, planning and building a church facility is usually many times the size of any house, and there are new building codes, accessibility codes, life-safety codes, zoning ordinances, and government bureaucrats to negotiate. Most church leaders were not trained to do this. Self-doubt is normal (and healthy to an extent); but with preparation, hard work, and godly wisdom, you can do what needs to be done.

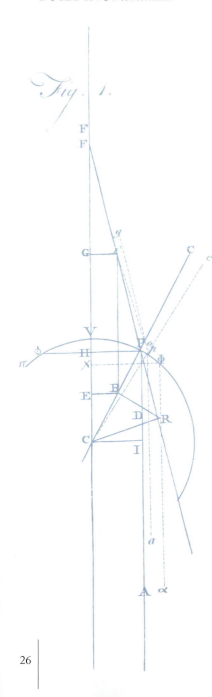

GIFTS FOR SERVICE

You have probably heard the old saying "God is not as concerned with your ability as your availability." Nehemiah observed this truth as the goldsmith became a stonemason and the rulers became roofers for a time. The perfumer made repairs as the priests built gates. God used their availability and gave them the ability. Knowing what they needed to know, God had prepared them for this day. You may not have been trained specifically for the task God has called you to, but He has been preparing you to use your skills to accomplish His purpose. He will supplement it with His ability where yours is lacking if you are faithful to do what He asks.

God gives gifts to those who are willing to act in obedience to His calling. He doesn't give gifts so that people can brag about them or put them on display. He gives you these gifts to use in service for Him. If you are called to a task, you can be sure God will make certain you have the gifts you need to complete it. Figuring out your gift is not as important as figuring out your calling. In fact, as in the case of Joshua at the Jordan River, sometimes God doesn't give the gift until we act.

This time Nehemiah's response was not to his enemies but directly to God. Although he was noticeably upset, he simply prayed to God and went on working. He asked God to "make their insults return on their own heads" (Neh. 4:4). Sometimes it is OK to get upset when people try to sidetrack you from God's work, but don't act on your anger. Take it to God and stay focused on the task at hand.

THE HALFWAY POINT

As Nehemiah's project reached the halfway point, we receive a key clue to the success of the project: "The people had the will to keep working" (Neh. 4:6). The will is a powerful thing. If the will is there, the people drive the project. They want to see it succeed. It is almost unstoppable. Two key tasks of a leader are: (1) to determine the right thing to do and (2) to stir up a desire in the people to do it.

There are a lot of ways to motivate people. Nehemiah explained the task and believed in it himself. Believing in the dream yourself is essential. It is also powerful and persuasive. That alone may not be enough in every situation. You will need to do your homework and make a case for why the project is the right course of action. Be prepared to provide an abundance of information and reasons not only for why you are convinced but also for why other ideas are not advisable. This is leadership. If you are not willing to commit to the idea, do not expect others to commit.

LEADERS GIVE DIRECTION

Without strong leadership even good people make bad decisions. A good spiritual leader tries to dissuade people from doing the wrong thing and tries to persuade them to do the right thing. But their will is still their own.

If the people are really behind a project, they will carry it forward. If they are not, they will stop at the first sign of resistance. People need strong leadership to give them the will to work. To help people believe in God's direction is an important step that cannot be underestimated, and is worthy of timely and thoughtful planning and implementation. The will to do the work is critical. Do not proceed until you have secured it.

THE OPPOSITION GETS STRONGER

Predictably, Sanballat and Tobiah came around again, this time with the Arabs, Ammonites, and Ashdodites. They had recruited more cynics to threaten the Israelites because they heard the work was progressing and the gaps were being closed up. They began planning to "come and fight against Jerusalem and throw it into confusion" (Neh. 4:8), but their threats were never carried out. The opposition's verbal attack, however, was effective. Rumors spread through the land that said, "We will never be able to rebuild the wall" (Neh. 4:10). The enemies' attempts to discourage and demoralize the workers were a constant battle for Nehemiah.

Without strong leadership even good people make bad decisions.

Your detractors will probably threaten "war" against you too. Like Nehemiah, keep working, and you may find that the project is finished and the war never starts. For some, however, war comes, so you must be prepared.

PREPARED FOR BATTLE

After an inspiring speech Nehemiah prepared his people for battle. He didn't keep the threats a secret; he rallied his people, preparing them to face the onslaught of the enemy. They wore swords as they worked. They held shields and spears as they took turns guarding the construction site. Nehemiah devised a plan to rally the people at the sound of the trumpet if an attack occurred. He and his fellow leaders were the most vigilant of all. They never took their clothes off, and they carried a weapon even when washing. And the work continued.

With this very real threat bearing down on the people, Nehemiah then found a new enemy, this one more damaging and threatening than the others. It was from within.

THE ENEMY WITHIN

Food was scarce as the Israelites began to stay inside the walls of the city. The farms were not producing, and the people had to mortgage their farms to eat while they were still paying taxes to the king. Even worse, their own people had begun to charge high interest rates on the money they borrowed to buy food. They were taking advantage of their brothers and sisters and making them slaves. As a good leader, Nehemiah wouldn't stand for this. He grew extremely angry at their greed. He confronted them directly, calling an assembly to address the issue. Those responsible recognized their sin when confronted with it and agreed to stop these practices.

Often we need to be made aware of how the things we are doing affect others. Sometimes it is the leaders' responsibility to help us see how our actions are affecting others

Leadership often means having the courage to do what is right and leaving the consequences up to God.

and to correct our behavior. This bad episode in the story of rebuilding the wall could have been much worse if Nehemiah had lacked the courage to confront these people with their sin. He had no guarantees that confrontation would work, but it was the right thing to do. Leadership often means having the courage to do what is right and leaving the consequences up to God.

Nehemiah's work continued to earn him respect. We see in Nehemiah 5:14 that he was appointed governor. However, he refused to live off the people. The taxes they paid went to the work of repairing the wall, and he and his associates never ate from the food allotted to the governor.

STAYING FOCUSED

As the project neared the end, Sanballat and the gang sent Nehemiah an invitation to meet with them. Sensing that they intended to harm him, he sent a great message: "I am doing a great work and cannot come down. Why should the work cease while I leave it and go down to you?" (Neh. 6:3).

Never let anything distract you from what God has called you to do. This is a hard lesson to learn but is essential for anyone in leadership. There will be hundreds of opportunities to be distracted from the work, to pursue worthwhile endeavors; but even good, positive things can be a diversion from the things God has called you to do.

Sanballat didn't ask for a meeting only once. He asked four times, and each time Nehemiah rejected the invitation. Finally, the fifth invitation became a threat. It said the men had heard rumors that the Jews were going to rebel and that Nehemiah wanted to be their king. They were probably the source of the rumors. They suggested that the king was going to hear these rumors, so he had better meet with them, presumably to negotiate. The reality was that they were going to try to kill Nehemiah.

Never violate the principles God has provided for you in Scripture.

ADVICE FROM FALSE PROPHETS

Keep in mind that when people come to you pledging to help with your project, they do not always have your best interest at heart. Some will take advantage of you and the church, given the opportunity. Be careful whom you trust. Con artists employed false prophets to try to get Nehemiah to go into the newly reconstructed temple to hide "because they are coming to kill you" (Neh. 6:10). Nehemiah wouldn't be tricked into violating the temple because he "realized that God had not sent him" (Neh. 6:12).

If God leads you to do something, it will never contradict the instruction of God's Word. Today we have the benefit of the whole Bible to speak into our lives and to help us understand and know what God wants us to do. Never violate the principles God has provided for you in Scripture. Whatever you do as a disciple and as a leader, whatever you lead your church to do, you should first test it against the principles that are taught throughout Scripture:

IS IT CONSISTENT WITH GOD'S LOVE?

IS IT BASED ON TRUTH?

IS IT BORN OF FAITH IN GOD OR ONLY OF HUMAN ABILITIES?

IS IT IN HARMONY WITH PATIENCE?

DOES IT MEASURE UP TO GOD'S STANDARD OF PEACE WITH OTHERS?

DOES IT SPEAK OF KINDNESS?

IS IT BASED ON SELF-CONTROL?

IS IT CONSISTENT WITH GOD'S FORGIVENESS?

These questions should be asked not only about the building itself but also about the process of planning in raising funds and enlisting support for the project. Are your methods consistent with the principles of obedience to God, truthfulness, good stewardship, benevolence, the Great Commission, and other scriptural concepts?

Only if the project is in complete harmony with the mind and heart of God can you expect Him to bless it. Because Scripture speaks to almost every situation, it can guide you in your decision making.

CELEBRATING SUCCESS

When the wall was finished, Nehemiah put his brother in charge of the city and conducted a census. The Levites read the Scriptures, and the people celebrated a feast, fasted, sacrificed, and dedicated themselves to obedience. They dedicated the wall by dividing into two groups, walking around it in opposite directions, and giving thanks.

THE WORK CONTINUES

Nehemiah found disobedience when he returned from a visit with the king. Tobias, of all people, had been given a place in the temple to store his things. This was a violation of the law of Moses, which the people had just pledged to uphold. Nehemiah saw people working the wine presses on the Sabbath. Jews had married women from Ashdod, Ammon, and Moab. Each transgression of the law had to be dealt with.

The work is not finished when the project is complete; it is just beginning. It is a joyful time to celebrate, but it is also a time to be diligent. To relax now and stop the work would negate the whole purpose of the construction project. So pace yourself and be ready to keep working when the building project is finished; there is more to come. In many ways, it is just the beginning.

King's Baptist
Church

SUN. SCH.   WORSHIP   PHONE
8:45AM   10AM & 6PM   597-3659
JOIN US IN WORSHIP
TWO MORNING SERVICES
8:45 AND 10:00

WWW.KINGSBAPTIST.ORG
3235

CHAPTER 2

The Challenge

You are about to undertake one of the most difficult tasks that any church leader can attempt.

Most survived and many even thrived through this challenging and strange process called a church building program, but some have tried and failed. Some got caught in the crossfire of bitter struggles between church members. Others discovered neighbors who regarded them as enemies and opposed them to the bitter end. Some neglected to consider the impact of legal and governmental controls. This book will attempt to help you navigate the complexities of a building program. We will analyze why some churches fail, but we will primarily focus on how to lead your church through the process in a way that will help bring success.

The Great Commission

The purpose of this book and of your project is not just to help your church build a building. There is a much greater purpose, driven by the Great Commission that Jesus issued: "All authority has been given to Me in heaven and on earth. Go, therefore, and make disciples of all nations, baptizing them in the name of the Father and of the Son and of the Holy Spirit, teaching them to observe everything I have commanded you. And remember, I am with you always, to the end of the age" (Matt. 28:18-20). We are commanded to go, make disciples, baptize, and teach. Building buildings is not in there! However, the building can be a means to this end. A building can be a great tool to help accomplish the Lord's command, or it can be a huge distraction and waste of resources. We must ensure it is the former and not the latter!

Success brings many rewards. One is the satisfaction of seeing a project come to reality. Another is the knowledge that the facilities you built will probably outlive you and will be used by future generations as a tool for ministry. Probably the greatest satisfaction is the reality that a well-built, well-designed, and wisely conceived building can enable your church to reach more people than ever before, people who otherwise would not have heard, seen, or believed if the building had not been completed.

Pastors and most lay leaders have limited experience with a building process. Building for the church is very different from building residential or even commercial construction. Relatively few have experienced what you are about to feel: the gaze of a thousand eyes focused on your work, some looking for flaws, some promoting their own agendas. Some will have the church's best interest at heart but may have a very different concept of what that should look like, based on their past experience.

You may have opposition. There will be challenges from many angles, and you will be stretched. There will be new language and terminology, new kinds of decisions to be made, possibly unscrupulous characters who will try to steer you away from the goal, and some challenges to your theology before you are finished. You will work with professionals you may have never dealt with before, as well as government agencies, zoning laws, rules, codes, ordinances, and regulations you have never heard of before.

So how can you better prepare yourself for a project like this? Too much is at risk to embark on this journey without preparation. That is the purpose of this book: to give you guidance in preparing yourself and your fellow leaders for the building process.

Spiritual Preparation

When successfully accomplished, the completion of a new facility can be a catalyst to launch a church into a new stage of existence. It can create a sense of excitement that catapults the church into more effective ministry, reaching more people and fulfilling its Kingdom purpose. Through the process of evaluating needs and planning a building project, a church can become more focused, have a clearer understanding of its priorities, and begin to do ministry better.

ZONING

The designation by a governing authority of the permissible use of a piece of property. Residential, multifamily, commercial, and industrial are examples of zoning designations. Churches are often allowed in any zoning area but may require a special-use permit to build in a certain zone.

The only reason the church should build is to further the cause of Christ, to allow the church to fulfill its mission.

However, churches can also let the building become the focus, allow money sources to drive the planning, or let its priorities get out of order. Then problems ensue. Churches that let the finances get out of hand find they are strapped for operating funds. Those that build a poor quality building, one that doesn't support ministry or one that is expensive to operate and maintain, find it robs them of resources. Planning and building a church facility is a difficult task that should not be undertaken without first considering the potential risks and making careful preparation.

The only reason the church should build is to further the cause of Christ, to allow the church to fulfill its mission. If that doesn't stir some serious opposition, nothing will. Anytime the church takes a bold step toward such a goal, it can expect opposition from those who would love to see it fail. The spiritual forces that hate the church will attack. It may be fierce and in your face, or it may be much more subtle; but it will come.

It is no surprise that churches set out on a course to build and receive attacks from all angles. It may be a spiritual battle, but it takes many forms, such as pastors becoming ill or other leaders being enticed toward selfish goals and away from the church's best interest. Moral failures can undercut the whole project and damage the fellowship. People fight with one another over seemingly unimportant things. Important issues meet with opposition from people and places we never would have anticipated. Agendas seemingly come from nowhere. Groups decide they no longer want to fellowship with certain others and dissolve the bonds that formed the congregation.

"Whoever thinks he stands must be careful not to fall!" (1 Cor. 10:12). As you undertake a construction project, prepare for battle and stay diligent. Lean heavily on Jesus. Stay close to Him, and His plan will come to pass. Jesus is even more interested in fulfilling the purpose of the church than you are. He will use you in ways you may not have dreamed of. His purpose is right. His design is perfect, and His motives are pure. You can count on Him to help you fight the spiritual battles that are ahead: "Be strengthened by the Lord and by His vast strength. Put on the full armor of God so that you can stand against the tactics of the Devil. For our battle is not against flesh and blood, but against the rulers, against the authorities, against the world powers of this darkness, against the spiritual forces of evil in the heavens. This is why you must take up the full armor of God, so that you may be able to resist in the evil day, and having prepared everything, to take your stand" (Eph. 6:10-13).

PREPARE YOUR HEART

You will not be effective in leading the church in the way God wants it to go if your relationship with God is clouded with unconfessed sin, disobedience, or an alternative agenda that can keep you from hearing God's voice clearly. No leader should try to lead a congregation through even the smallest project without proper preparation. You wouldn't preach a sermon without studying. You wouldn't host a dinner party without planning the menu, nor would you go on a long trip without planning your route and packing the things you need. So you must prepare for this journey as well. To be the most usable tool in God's hands, it is imperative that you first empty yourself of all that might cloud your judgment or divert your attention from His perfect will.

Spiritual preparation always begins with emptying yourself so that God can fill you. It starts with confession. Before asking God to use you, you first must be cleansed of the things that you have allowed to come between you and our Lord. Claiming 1 John 1:9, ask for forgiveness of "the sin that so easily ensnares" you (see Heb. 12:1).

Be specific. Be ruthless. Don't make excuses! God knows exactly what you need to confess; ask Him to bring it to your mind. Then respond with humility and honesty before God. Through brokenness over your sin, a genuine feeling of remorse for allowing these things to intrude into your relationship with Him, you can be in a better posture to hear the whispers of the Spirit.

If you make excuses or hold on to something because "it isn't that bad," you are presenting an opportunity for the enemy to gain a foothold and attack. You must get rid of anything that would distract you from what God wants to accomplish through you.

CLEANSE THROUGH CONFESSION

Confess your hatred, pride, selfishness, ambition, lust, jealousy, greed, anger, impatience, and lack of self-control. Name your sins and confess your inability to overcome them in your own strength. Ask God, through the strength of His Spirit, to overcome these things in your life and to keep you from falling into your old habits again. Claim Philippians 4:13: "I am able to do all things through Him who strengthens me."

DEAL WITH PRIDE. In Proverbs 8:13 God says, "I hate arrogant pride." Why? Because pride can cloud our vision and cause us to do things to draw attention to ourselves rather than Jesus. The desire to be recognized and admired by our peers and others causes us to do the wrong things or to do the right things in the wrong way or for the wrong reason. The components of a building project—its design, promotion, funding, and the attention it will bring—are perfect opportunities for a leader's pride to creep in and divert energy away from Kingdom priorities.

The decision of what to include in a building can easily be influenced by pride. Because of pride a staff member tells himself he deserves a bigger office, a teacher claims the classroom with the best view, the pastor thinks of the design of the building as a way to bring attention to himself, the big giver in the capital fund-raising campaign thinks his gift makes him more important, or the chairman of the building committee enjoys being in the limelight. All of these can be motivated by selfish pride and make the project more vulnerable to attack.

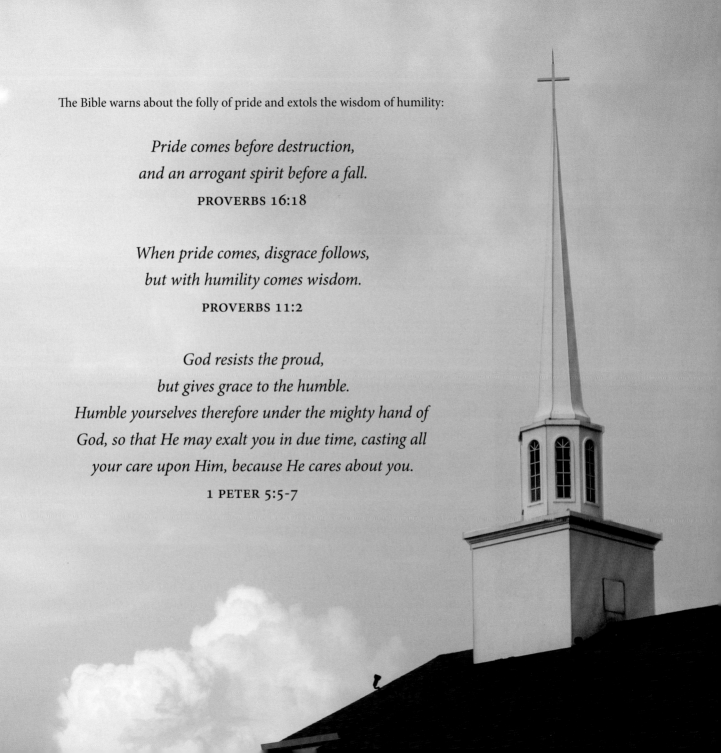

The Bible warns about the folly of pride and extols the wisdom of humility:

Pride comes before destruction,
and an arrogant spirit before a fall.

PROVERBS 16:18

When pride comes, disgrace follows,
but with humility comes wisdom.

PROVERBS 11:2

God resists the proud,
but gives grace to the humble.
Humble yourselves therefore under the mighty hand of
God, so that He may exalt you in due time, casting all
your care upon Him, because He cares about you.

1 PETER 5:5-7

To prepare for the project ahead, take a few moments to confess your pride and to ask God to rid you of selfish ambition. Do it now.

Ask God to prepare your heart and open your mind to His guidance and direction.

Set aside all of your vain desires and ego-driven schemes to get ahead.

Ask God to allow His will to penetrate your mind and overwhelm your desires.

Ask God to put to death the selfishness and vanity that would cloud your vision and compromise this project.

In its place ask God to fill you with His desires and vision for this project.

Setting aside self and focusing on God and His glory, earnestly seek His wisdom and direction and let His agenda, not yours, dominate the conversation.

Hebrews 12:1-2 instructs us to put our focus on Jesus: "Since we also have such a large cloud of witnesses surrounding us, let us lay aside every weight and the sin that so easily ensnares us, and run with endurance the race that lies before us, keeping our eyes on Jesus, the source and perfecter of our faith, who for the joy that lay before Him endured a cross and despised the shame, and has sat down at the right hand of God's throne" (Heb. 12:1-2). The sin that ensnares could refer to pride. The writer instructs us to lay that aside and replace it with a focused life. Only by fixing our eyes on Jesus can we hope to keep from falling back into the selfish and prideful ways we are all prone to.

Think of Jesus' redemptive work and the price He paid for our salvation. Maintaining a focus on Jesus' sacrifice will help keep you humble and intent on exalting Him. When thoughts of Jesus and His sacrifice fill your mind, you can more easily stay focused on the task of bringing others to Him.

CLEANSE YOUR HEART. For God to use us, we must have a clean heart:

Who may ascend the mountain of the LORD?
Who may stand in His holy place?
The one who has clean hands and a pure heart,
who has not set his mind on what is false,
and who has not sworn deceitfully.
He will receive blessing from the LORD,
and righteousness from the God of his salvation.

PSALM 24:3-5

What other sin do you need to confess to be purified and to prepare for the spiritual battle ahead? If you have sin in your life that you are unwilling to confess and abandon, you are in no shape to take on a building project. The good news is that when we confess our sin, "He is faithful and righteous to forgive us our sins and to cleanse us from all unrighteousness" (1 John 1:9).

To confess simply means to agree with God that it is sin and that you are willing to give it up for Him. Trust Him to do the cleansing. Then do what Jesus told the woman caught in adultery: "Go, and from now on do not sin any more" (John 8:11). Don't think your sin isn't that bad. To be really clean, clean enough to lead others, you will need to be broken over your sin, understanding that it could provide an opportunity for your spiritual enemy to sneak in and undermine the whole project. Ask yourself, *Has God told me to do something I have been postponing or am unwilling to do?* Disobedience clouds your communication with God. How can you expect Him to make more of His will clear to you when you have not obeyed what you already know to be His will?

It is likely that at some point in the process of planning and building, conflict will arise. Your patience may be tested. A church leader must not hold a grudge. You may need to offer forgiveness to others who do not agree with you or who have wronged you. Forgiveness is an act of your will to let go of others' wrongs. To fail to forgive can build up resentment and barriers in your relationships, yet it is important that all of your relationships be healthy during a building program. Ask God to teach you to forgive and to give you the strength to let go of resentment. Don't let holding on to transgressions harm your ability to communicate and make better decisions.

Finally, rid your mind of any agenda other than seeking God's will for your church. Even though spiritual motives led you to plan a certain type of building, include certain features, or exclude certain others, leave room for the Holy Spirit to come through with a totally different agenda. His agenda is the only one that is really important.

Forget promises that may have been made in haste. Lay aside things you have always thought should be included in the next building project. You no longer represent a special-interest group in the church; rather, you must become a leader, totally committed to discovering and doing God's will. It takes selflessness, humility, and wisdom.

Stop and spend time in spiritual preparation. Confess your sin—big things as well as little things you might otherwise overlook. Bring them to the altar and ask God to remove them. Ask Him to take away your taste for sinful acts and improper thoughts. Ask Him to bring to mind what you need to confess; respond by doing so quickly. Don't argue with the Spirit; just agree with Him, confess it, and accept forgiveness.

Ask God to bring to mind things you have been disobedient about and resolve to obey now. Ask Him to cleanse your mind of any agenda that might prejudice your thoughts. Ask Him to prepare you for the task at hand. If you want God's best for your church, if you want to find His will, if you want to position yourself to be the leader your church needs to take them through this process, then pray for Him to cleanse your soul and prepare you for the leadership role that is before you.

TRUST GOD'S PREPARATION

If God has placed you in this role to lead His church in a building project, He has surely prepared you for it. As God prepared Moses in the wilderness for 40 years, He has been preparing you for the task before you.

Moses was a slow-speaking alien shepherd in the desert when God called him to lead. But it was his time in the desert that prepared him to lead an entire nation of people out of Egypt, through the desert, and to—although not into—the promised land.

God has been preparing you. Whether or not you know it, He has been sharpening your skills and giving you what you need for the task. Slow to speak? No problem! Lack experience? Moses had never led people, just sheep! Need wisdom? God has plenty! There is nothing you could need for the journey that God cannot provide.

If you feel you are in over your head, good! You probably are, but God says, "Do not be afraid or discouraged, for the LORD your God is with you wherever you go" (Josh. 1:9). He will be there to guide you and be your leader, even as you lead.

You no longer represent a special-interest group in the church; rather, you must become a leader, totally committed to discovering and doing God's will.

THE INTERCEDING LEADER

The Israelites had been walking in the wilderness for more than two years—two years of fighting and plagues, two years of straying away and worshiping other gods, two years of faithful and miraculous provision for their needs, two years of complaining and murmuring. The Lord told Moses to send scouts to see the land they were going to conquer and own. It seems the Lord wanted to give His people something to look forward to. They needed reassurance that following Moses all over the desert was worth it because someday they would inhabit a land that was rich and fertile.

The scouts returned with a report that must have been the disappointment of the century. The fruit was enormous, and the land was fertile and "flowing with milk and honey"; but the land was occupied by huge men who would see them as grasshoppers (Num. 13:27). However, one of the scouts, Caleb, gave a different report: "We must go up and take possession of the land because we can certainly conquer it!" (Num. 13:30).

The entire camp erupted into tears. At this point they were ready to select a new leader and return to Egypt. But there was a little encouragement: Caleb was behind Moses and believed God would deliver the land to them. (He was not to realize this for some time, but God was faithful to him and saw that Caleb got his land.) As for Moses, he kept on with a few leaders who were faithful. Aaron, Joshua, Caleb, and he pleaded with the people not to turn back. Numbers 14:10 says at that point "the whole community threatened to stone them."

Meanwhile, God was about to wipe out the Israelites and start over. Even He was sick and tired of their complaining. But Moses pleaded with God, asking Him to "please pardon the wrongdoing of this people in keeping with the greatness of Your faithful love, just as You have forgiven them from Egypt until now" (Num. 14:19). That's right. Moses pleaded with the people not to turn their backs on God, then turned right around and pleaded with God not to wipe them out for their sin. This is the role of a leader who faces a crisis: he encourages the people to do the right thing and petitions

God on their behalf to have mercy and patience with their lack of faith when they aren't obedient. This intercessory role is not for someone who has his own agenda, pride, and burden of sin to carry. This person must be a true leader, a humble servant leader who desires what is best for the people he is leading.

Moses and Aaron humbled themselves before the people, begging them to do the right thing: "Moses and Aaron fell down with their faces to the ground in front of the whole assembly of the Israelite community" (Num. 14:5). No pride there! Moses and Aaron had pure faith that God was the real deal. They knew God would deliver on His promise if the Israelites would give Him a chance.

CHOOSE YOUR ADVISERS CAREFULLY

Moses was fortunate to have a few fellow leaders to support him and encourage him. He had chosen his leaders carefully, and he knew whom to listen to.

As a leader, you may have to stand and plead your case to God and/or to your people. How important would it be to have an Aaron, a Joshua, and a Caleb to stand with you? You need advisers who share your vision and goals:

> *Plans fail when there is no counsel,*
> *but with many advisers they succeed.*
> **PROVERBS 15:22**

As you prepare to lead in a building project, pray for your fellow leaders. Pray for wisdom in choosing whom you will listen to. You will get all sorts of advice, some of it good and some of it terrible. Knowing the character of those who surround you and the soundness of their advice is extremely important.

This is the role of a leader who faces a crisis: he encourages the people to do the right thing and petitions God on their behalf to have mercy and patience with their lack of faith when they aren't obedient.

If you surround yourself with worldly businesspersons who are not spiritual, you will get unspiritual advice. Even Jesus was careful about the people He trusted: "While He was in Jerusalem at the Passover Festival, many trusted in His name when they saw the signs He was doing. Jesus, however, would not entrust Himself to them, since He knew them all and because He did not need anyone to testify about man; for He Himself knew what was in man" (John 2:23-25).

You will need discernment about whom you invite to give you advice. Know whom you are listening to and whom you are giving control to. God wants your church to succeed, but He will not violate scriptural principles to make it happen. Depend on men and women who will keep you honest, do the right thing, and use great wisdom in discovering the way God wants to lead you.

Before you listen to advice, consider its source. Ask:

ARE THESE PERSONS MOTIVATED to see the church succeed or to bring themselves more wealth, more comfort, or more glory?

DOES THEIR LIFESTYLE AND CONDUCT REVEAL their commitment to Christ? If not, why would their advice be worthwhile?

MIGHT THEY HAVE AN AGENDA to sell something or to personally gain from their recommendation?

DO THEY TRULY HAVE KNOWLEDGE about the subject, or do they have only strong feelings about what should be done?

WOULD YOU BE ASHAMED TO STAND BEFORE GOD and say you took action based on these persons' recommendations?

SEEK WISDOM

You will need wisdom to go forward in your project. You can read books, talk to others who have built, hire professionals, and talk to denominational leaders, but you will probably get conflicting advice. True wisdom comes from God.

Happy is a man who finds wisdom
and who acquires understanding.

PROVERBS 3:13

Wisdom is better than precious stones,
and nothing desirable can compare with it.

PROVERBS 8:11

The fear of the Lord *is the beginning of wisdom,*
and the knowledge of the Holy One is understanding.

PROVERBS 9:10

You will not be likely to get wisdom from advisers who have their own agendas, such as salesmen and immature believers. You may not even get it from experienced professionals. So where can you go to get godly wisdom? First and foremost, it is in the Bible. Let Scripture speak to your situation. Let the priorities of Scripture become the priorities for your construction project.

What are these? When Jesus was asked which is the greatest commandment, His reply was "Love the Lord your God with all your heart, with all your soul, and with all your mind. This is the greatest and most important commandment. The second is like it: Love your neighbor as yourself" (Matt. 22:37-39).

Later Jesus gave another commandment to His followers: "Go, therefore, and make disciples of all nations, baptizing them in the name of the Father and of the Son and of the Holy Spirit, teaching them to observe everything I have commanded you. And remember, I am with you always, to the end of the age" (Matt. 28:19-20).

So there you have it: love God, love others, make disciples. Of course, the hard part is to translate these priorities into buildings; but as long as you have these ideas in mind, you should always be able to ask yourself how each decision you are making would impact your ability to obey Christ's commands.

FOCUS ON THE BIG PICTURE

As you think about the building project, try to gain a broad perspective of its impact on the whole ministry of the church and on the kingdom of God. Too often churches see their project as an isolated task, such as building a family-life center.

Everything you do in regard to buildings and property has an effect on the entire church. If you place a building anywhere on the property, that location is one place you

cannot put another building, parking, landscaping, or other features. It also absorbs financial resources that are no longer available for other projects.

For this reason the best leaders look at projects from a big-picture viewpoint. Seek the answers to questions like these:

WHAT OTHER FACILITIES might be needed in the future?

HOW CAN THE CURRENT PROJECT relate to both existing and future facilities?

COULD THIS PROJECT deplete some resources that will soon be needed by a higher-priority ministry project?

One of the best ways to answer these questions is to obtain a comprehensive master plan. We will discuss this further in a later chapter. The point here is to keep a broad view of the project.

DON'T NEGLECT YOUR OTHER RESPONSIBILITIES

If you are like most leaders in the church, you do many jobs. Leading a building project will add to the other responsibilities you have, making it more difficult to balance your life. Lay leaders must balance their personal lives with their vocations and their church responsibilities. Very few leaders have the luxury of putting their careers on hold while they lead a church building program.

You will need a clear set of priorities to avoid burning out or dropping the ball on a critical task. You must consider the building project from the perspective of all the church is doing and all you are doing. Certainly, the project is very important; but so is teaching a Sunday School class or leading a women's Bible study.

If you are a pastor, there is no more important job than proclaiming the gospel. The building project cannot be allowed to distract you from such a priority task. The work of the church cannot be placed on hold while you plan the building and carry out its construction. Do not allow a building project to displace the evangelistic mission of the church. They can happen simultaneously.

If you are not the pastor but another leader, it is partly your responsibility to help the pastor so that he is not overwhelmed by the construction project. His leadership is vital, but he should not be the only one leading. He should have strong leaders to step up and accept their share of the load so that his part is bearable. Be sensitive to the state of balance among all of the parties involved in the building program. If things get too demanding, the project may need to slow down.

At the same time, a church construction project is important enough to make it a priority over some other things. It is important that the project keeps moving and maintains some momentum through the process. The leader must be able to give the project the time it deserves to sustain movement.

When a project stalls, a lot can be lost. The church begins to wonder how important it really is. Is it worth a financial sacrifice on their part if it seems it is not a priority to the leadership? When there is no perceptible movement, the congregation will assume the leadership has lost interest. This may be far from the truth, but it would be hard to persuade an outsider otherwise.

If you are a pastor, there is no more important job than proclaiming the gospel.

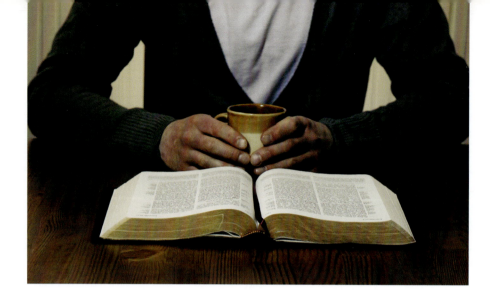

PRAYER IS ESSENTIAL

Another key to finding true wisdom is through prayer. Ask for wisdom. James 1:5 says, "If any of you lacks wisdom, he should ask God, who gives to all generously and without criticizing, and it will be given to him." God's will is not some hidden thing that only a genius can figure out. God wants us to know and do His will. If we ask and seek His will for this project with the intent to obey whatever He wants, He will reveal it. Conversely, don't expect God to reveal His will to those who have no intention to obey.

You will find many other things and people to pray about through the planning and building process:

PRAY FOR CHURCH MEMBERS to have wisdom. Pray for them to be open to God's will.

PRAY FOR THE PROFESSIONALS you will be working with to design the building (the architect and engineers, for example).

PRAY FOR THE GENERAL CONTRACTOR AND SUBCONTRACTORS who will work on the construction project.

PRAY FOR THE ZONING, BUILDING, AND FIRE OFFICIALS who will sign the permits to build your project.

PRAY FOR THE PASTOR AND STAFF of your church as they continue doing their normal ministry along with the added stress and responsibility of a building project.

PRAY FOR YOUR FELLOW LEADERSHIP-TEAM MEMBERS and the rest of the congregation to be united in their desire to find God's will and to build according to His plan.

PRAY FOR A LOVING SPIRIT IN THE CHURCH as you tackle difficult questions and deal with decisions and choices that must be made.

PRAY FOR THE BANKERS AND FINANCIERS who will lend you money for the project.

PRAY FOR THE CAPITAL-CAMPAIGN LEADERS you will hire to help the church grow in stewardship and lead your people through a capital . program with a strong spiritual dimension.

PRAY FOR THE GENEROSITY OF CHURCH MEMBERS and others who will give liberally to fund the project and continue to support the ongoing work of the church.

PRAY FOR THE MINISTRY that will take place in the new facilities.

PRAY FOR FAVORABLE WEATHER during critical construction periods.

PRAY FOR THE IMPACT the project can have on the community by attracting new families and gaining favor and respect for the church.

PRAY FOR THE EFFECT THE BUILDING can have on church members, giving them a sense of excitement and enthusiasm that will encourage them to invite friends.

Prepare the Congregation

One role of a leader is not only to be in the right place doing the right thing but also to convince others to do the same. It often takes a gifted communicator to get others to deny their own will and conform to God's.

Don't assume the congregation understands that the Great Commission drives the building process. Spell it out for them: the goal is to reach people and to grow numerically. Be prepared to explain the following truths.

GOD wants your church to grow, and the church desires this growth as well.

THE CHURCH can be effective at reaching the mission field.

THE CHURCH is committed to do what it takes to accomplish growth, including providing facilities to sustain and support balanced growth.

With this foundation a plan can be developed to lead the church into the future with confidence.

If the congregation does not yet share these commitments, you have some work to do to get them ready. The Bible is full of examples of people who did not want to go where God was leading; but through leaders like Moses, Aaron, David, Nehemiah, Ezra, Deborah, and Jeremiah, He was able to move them to where He wanted them to be.

THE BUILDING IS NOT THE CHURCH

Early in the process it is important to lay down some ground rules about the building-planning process, both in design-team meetings and in ongoing dialogue with the congregation. If the congregation judges the design of the new building by a standard other than the Great Commission or has the misconception that the building is the church, they will come up with very different conclusions about what is best for the church. Confusing the institution with the church breeds all kinds of problems. If a building needs to be replaced or the church must relocate to a new site, members who think the church is the building can be greatly disturbed. Beyond the sentimental attachment and memories that naturally go with the geographical location of the church facility, they will think you are destroying the church as they know it.

Most leaders have a clear understanding that the building is not the church. It is just the house the church meets in. In fact, for this reason the old-fashioned term *church house* is an accurate way to refer to the building. This truth needs to be taught and retaught to your congregation. You might be surprised to learn how often you hear people refer to a building program as "building a new church," especially if it includes a worship facility. Throughout the process teach your church these truths.

THE CHURCH is made up of its members.

THE BUILDING is just a meeting house.

THE CHURCH is the body of Christ.

THE CHURCH is the bride of Christ.

Reinforcing these biblical truths about the church will provide perspective about the purpose of the building program and will help prevent confusion. Continually teach these truths as you talk about the project. This message will need to be repeated many

The church is made up of its members.

times and in different ways for it to sink in. Be persistent and gently correct team members who forget. The building process can be an opportunity to teach the congregation about the nature of the church, stewardship principles, and much more.

THE COMFORT OF MEMBERS IS NOT THE GOAL

Some church members seem to think the church is building a facility to make its members more comfortable. Perhaps things are getting a little crowded, the nursery is outdated, or the fellowship hall is too small for your fellowships. These might seem to be good reasons to build, but the church cannot lose sight of the Great Commission.

Most evangelical churches that build are doing so with one primary goal in mind: to reach more people for Christ. Herein is a key question: Who are the people the church will reach in the future? Are they like the current members? Younger? Older? Of child-bearing age? Students? Empty nesters? Will they be on the same economic level of current members? Richer or poorer? Will they be better educated? More professional? Blue collar? Ethnically diverse? Is the area around the church changing? How will that affect the answer to these questions?

The answers to these questions are very important for this reason: you are designing the building for people who are not currently members. Therefore, you must know something about them in order to design the kind of space that meets the needs of them and their families.

The economic status of your constituency makes a difference in the quality and aesthetics necessary to reach that demographic most effectively. The educational levels usually affect the types of programs you will offer. The ages to be reached may impact the relative size and growth rate of the preschool and children's Sunday School space.

A STEWARDSHIP MIND-SET

As a leader and as a congregation, the way you view finances can greatly influence the way the project is carried out. Principles of stewardship need to be taught throughout the life of the church, but they become a very practical matter when it is time to build.

If church members have not learned that all resources belong to God, the ownership of the building can become a contentious issue. If people treat a space as if it belonged to them and not to God and certainly not to the rest of the congregation, they might have a difficult time when it comes time to redistribute the space to allow for growth. The truth that God blesses a cheerful giver, the difference between tithing and giving, and believers' responsibility for using resources are all essential foundational understandings for good decision making.

The balance between faith and presumption is a difficult concept for most people to understand. When you start talking about the projected cost of the building and the feasibility of the project, someone might ask, "Why worry about the cost? God will pay for it!" Yet the Bible emphasizes counting the cost of an endeavor in addition to having faith in God. We must be accountable for the cost of the building project. Jesus said in Luke 14:28, "Which of you, wanting to build a tower, doesn't first sit down and calculate the cost to see if he has enough to complete it?"

God holds us accountable for the resources he entrusts to us.

Teach the congregation financial accountability as Jesus taught it in the parable of the talents in Matthew 25. There Jesus recounted the story of a master who gave each of his servants a different amount of money to manage. To one he gave 5 talents, to another he gave 2, and to the other he gave 1; then he left town. On his return the master called for an accounting of the trust he had made. The servant who had been given 5 talents had invested it and had earned 5 more. He said to this servant, "Well done, good and faithful slave! You were faithful over a few things; I will put you in charge of many things. Share your master's joy!" (v. 21). The second servant had also wisely invested and doubled his money, meriting his master's praise.

However, the servant who had been given only 1 talent had said to himself, *My master is hard and reaps where he does not sow.* So he had buried the talent he had been given and returned it to the master just as it was. The master took the talent from that servant and gave it to the good steward who had 10 talents, saying, "You evil, lazy slave! If you knew that I reap where I haven't sown and gather where I haven't scattered, then you should have deposited my money with the bankers. And when I returned I would have received my money with interest" (vv. 26-27). This parable teaches us several things about the way we are to use the resources God has entrusted to us.

WE ARE ACCOUNTABLE. God holds us accountable for the resources he entrusts to us. Whether we are given much or little material wealth, we are accountable for the way we use the resources God has given us.

WE ARE TO INVEST WISELY. Having little is no excuse. The master was not concerned about how little or how much the stewards invested but about whether they invested wisely. In fact, usually the more you invest, the greater the potential return for the investment. The servant with 5 talents could have risked only 2 or 3, keeping the rest in reserve in case the investment went bad. Instead, he risked it all. By investing only 3, he would have gained only 3. By investing all 5, he earned 5 more.

Some churches and/or church members seem to have the idea that spending less is somehow more spiritual than spending more, that the less you spend on a building, the better it is for the kingdom of God. The lavishness of the Old Testament temple indicates that God was not very interested in holding down the price.

This parable shows us that God wants us to preserve His resources but that we must also be willing to risk them for His kingdom, wisely and with purpose. Investing a small amount can mean small results. A big investment might mean big results but only if we invest in something that yields a good return. An unwise investment means we throw away the money God has provided.

WE EXPECT TO EARN A RETURN ON OUR INVESTMENT. This parable of the talents reminds us of the difference between investment and spending. When we invest, we expect to receive a return on our investment. When we invest in a building project, we expect returns like the following.

> *Spiritual growth* of current and future church members
>
> *Numerical growth* of the congregation
>
> *Ministry expansion* as the needs of the church and community are met more effectively
>
> *Multiplied missions* as more lost people are reached with the good news of Jesus

These returns on our investment—lives changed and the Kingdom expanded—make the risk of our resources worthwhile. On the other hand, if we don't expect such a return, why build? It would be wiser to invest that money where it will produce fruit.

A sound stewardship mind-set includes using facilities efficiently. It is desirable and often necessary to consider using space multiple times. The multiple uses of space can entail using the same room for fellowship and adult classrooms with movable walls. It may mean eating in a gym or even worshiping in one for a time.

Sharing space, the multiple uses of space, and having multiple worship services are ways to make the most of space. Your planning should include decisions about how much and what type of multiple uses you should employ, but don't overlook this important tool as you create new ways to reach people.

BUILDINGS DON'T REACH PEOPLE

A common error you might hear is "All we have to do is build a building, and people will come!" You may have heard this from new church plants that assume their lack of a building is hampering growth. It has also been espoused by old, established churches that need or want to build and are trying to make their case. But the prevalence of half-empty buildings across the United States testifies to the falsehood of that statement.

Your church may grow after it builds a building, but it will not be the building that causes the growth. Churches grow when they minister to the needs of people. Having an "If we build it, they will come," *Field of Dreams* attitude can backfire on you. People soon realize that buildings don't cause growth.

But there is often a connection between the completion of a building and a burst of growth in the church. A new building can allow a church to experience significant growth if certain conditions are in place:

GROWTH HAS BEEN LIMITED by the facilities and the church does a good job of presenting itself and the new construction to the community.

THE CHURCH BUILDS the right kind of space that creates balance in its capacity, making it possible for the church to grow in all areas.

THE CHURCH KEEPS DOING the things that produced growth in the first place.

Many churches grow significantly before they ever build their first facility. Saddleback Community Church in Orange County, California, met in 15 different locations and grew to about 10,000 in attendance before it built its first permanent building.

If the church is not growing, a new building may or may not begin a new growth trend. It depends on what other factors are limiting the church's growth. If there are problems in the fellowship, staff problems, leadership problems, or other factors, a building will not solve them. A new set of tires will not make your car run any better if it needs new spark plugs. You can spend a lot of money trying to solve the wrong problem. The lack of space can limit the growth of a church, but the mere presence of space cannot be expected to cause growth.

Only people can reach people. Once the building is complete, the people of the church must put it to work to reach people. They must lead the new classes that will meet in the new classrooms that have been built. They must fill the new choir loft, help with parking, greet new people at the welcome center, and take other leadership roles. Church members' willingness to serve, share, and reach out are the factors that produce growth. The building simply creates a place for these things to happen.

*Only people can
reach people.*

CHAPTER 3

Getting Started

Facilities can be extremely important
to the mission of your church.

Buildings: Three Views

We will use three illustrations to help your team understand ways your church can utilize space to reach its goals.

THE CHURCH FACILITY AS A CONTAINER

The church is like a container. It is the envelope around your ministries. Of course, the building does not contain all of the ministries of the church. The church ministers in your home, at school, at your office, at mission sites, and around the world; however, the church facility houses your base of operations. It gives you an identity and a tangible presence in the community.

Most churches design their facility to contain the core ministries of the church—the ongoing ministries that require specialized space and/or dedicated space to do them well. This design is one way we communicate the priorities of the church. If it is important, we provide for it. We invest in it so that we can do it well.

The idea of the facility as a container presents problems for churches that don't have on-campus Bible study like Sunday School because the nonverbal message is that they don't regard small groups as a core ministry. The churches then have to constantly counter this false message. Such churches usually have about 50 to 60 percent of their worshipers involved in Bible study, while many traditional churches with dedicated facilities and a balanced capacity for growth frequently have 75 to 80 percent involved. Churches with on-campus Bible study have developed a culture of discipleship. The priority placed on Bible study is clearly reinforced by the allotment of space.

HAVE THE RIGHT SIZED CONTAINER. Depending on how your church does ministry, you need the right amount of space to contain the ministries you determine should be housed at this facility. For most churches this means worship services and some educational programs such as Sunday School will be housed here. Along with these you will need adequate parking.

Balance is the key. If you want your church to be healthy, strive for balance. The worship attendance needs to balance with the educational attendance. Having the right capacity in the facility is crucial for this attendance to happen. Balance does not usually mean equal. It varies according to your strategy and philosophy of ministry. If you are pleased to have 60 percent of those attending worship involved in small groups, that can be your goal. Others might strive toward 80 percent or more. It's up to you.

Be aware, however, that whenever you run out of a certain type of space, your facility will begin to constrain the growth of that aspect of ministry. If you build a large worship area but only token Sunday School space, either the church will become unbalanced with a lack of discipleship, or the entire church, including the worship attendance, will be constrained by the lack of educational space.

Which of these occurs will most likely be determined by the culture of the church. If it is a new church, the culture is just being formed, and it will become normal to have only a few in Sunday School compared to worship attendance.

Make allowances for growth in all programs and age groups.

The balance between the two will be heavily weighted toward worship, and the expectation to attend Sunday School will be discounted by the nonverbal communication of the lack of space. If the church culture is already established with a strong Sunday School program, the entire organization will usually be constrained by the amount of educational space provided. No program will typically outgrow the capacity of the Sunday School space provided by more than a few percent.

ALLOW ROOM TO GROW. When designing a building, make allowances for growth in all programs and age groups. The amount of growth capacity needed above the existing attendance can vary greatly, depending on the growth potential of the ministry area and the priority the church has placed on growth.

Any container has a limit. For example, we can place apples in a bowl until it gets full, then continue to pile them on top until they start to roll out. It doesn't matter how fast we add apples if the bowl can't hold more. A container can hold only a certain amount of growth. The same is true of your facility. At some point it reaches the limit of growth it can contain. You either get another bowl or a bigger bowl, or you limit the growth.

Some churches continue to grow well beyond the limit of their facility. How do we account for this fact? Is the container full, or does it not have the effect of limiting growth for some reason? Growth is not necessarily stopped cold at the moment of saturation. There might be sufficient momentum in the church to continue growing for some period of time, to stretch the envelope. But even such a church will eventually feel the effects of saturated space. The lack of growth space constrains growth. It may not stop it, but it will certainly make growth more difficult.

To a rapidly growing church with a lot of momentum, the effects might be gradual; but for a church with little or no momentum, space limitations can stop growth immediately or prevent it from ever occurring. A church that has plateaued or even begun to lose members will not usually have the momentum to overcome space limitations.

I have visited many churches that stopped growing long ago, having lost all of their momentum. Restarting the growth curve in an upward direction will take a significant effort. These churches do not need the additional obstacle of a lack of space to stand in the way of renewed growth.

Even a healthy, growing church does not want to throw an obstacle in the way of growth. Although the church may be able to overcome it, the church has also expended energy and effort that might have been used for other ministry. How much more effective could that church be without the limitation of inadequate space?

NO HOLES! This principle is true for every area of church ministry. Each aspect of the church program, if it is a priority, needs room to grow. Within the Sunday School organization, each age group and each class has its limit. If you run out of preschool space, it doesn't matter that you may still have room in the adult men's class. The lack of preschool space constrains the church's overall growth. Even if there is an almost empty room elsewhere in the building, you can't put preschoolers in the adult men's class. Neither group would be happy!

Trying to grow the church with a lack of space in one area would be like trying to fill a bucket with a hole in it. The water will rise only to the level of the hole. In the same way, your organization will rise only to the level allowed by the age group that runs out of space first. Be sure your building doesn't have any such holes built into the design!

THE CHURCH FACILITY AS A BILLBOARD

Billboards are large signs along the road that communicate a message to passersby about a product or an event. Similarly, your church building tells people what your church is like. Although hopefully a lot more attractive than most billboards, the building design communicates a nonverbal message about the church's priorities and values.

Written on your billboard are the values, attitudes, and vision of your church. To the people driving by, the message is not written in words; but it can be seen in the shape and size of the building, the way it is landscaped and maintained, and the openness of the layout. It is in the availability of parking and the clarity of where to enter the building. It is on the signage around the church property. Is your church communicating a message of "Do not enter" or "Welcome"?

COMMUNICATING VALUES. If you gave someone a piece of jewelry in a brown envelope, the wrapping would not suggest that the gift was very valuable. But if you put that same piece of jewelry in an attractive, custom-made box lined with velvet, covered with beautiful wrapping paper, and tied up with a bow, the impression would be that this gift is something of great value. In the same way, your church building suggests that something of great or little value is inside.

The way the building and your ministry are perceived also depends on the perspective of the viewer who sees your campus. A simple and plain church building might communicate to one passerby that this congregation is not concerned with the external but only with the eternal and thus be attractive to him. But another person might think the same facility communicates a lack of respect for the message. He might reason, *They don't respect the God they claim to believe in enough to build a decent building. How could they possibly offer anything of value to me?* To him, the building would suggest that the church doesn't value its relationship with God, and he would be repulsed.

A large, elaborate building with beautiful lines and costly materials would give a different impression, but the perception would still depend on the viewer. It might impress and attract one viewer, while another might see the church as too concerned with outward appearance. Each building makes its own impression and sends its own message, and each person interprets the message according to his or her own values and taste. Every part of what a person sees and experiences combines to make an over-all impression. Observers then decide to visit the church or conclude it is not their kind of church, often without ever crossing the threshold.

YET BUILDINGS CAN LIE TOO! Sometimes a building sends a false message. To someone passing by, the building communicates that the church is not only traditional but also stuck in the past. Stepping into your building is like stepping through a time warp to the 1950s or 1960s. But the reality may be that your ministry is very relevant and is not doing church the same way it was done in the 1950s. Many churches want to update their facility so that its message is in harmony with the reality behind those walls.

People in the community can miss the impact of your ministry if your building doesn't reveal the truth of what it has to offer. Your goal is to have an exterior that is inviting to a broad spectrum of people and a church that is alive and vibrant on the inside.

TARGETING POPULATION SEGMENTS. Occasionally, a church may want to build with the intent to target a segment of the population that would be attracted by a particular type of building. In doing so, the church runs the risk of failing to reach other segments of the population, but that may or may not be a problem. In these situations the problem can come later if the church decides to take another direction. If the facilities are too geared toward one group, it can be difficult to broaden the ministry later.

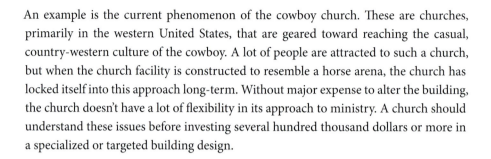

An example is the current phenomenon of the cowboy church. These are churches, primarily in the western United States, that are geared toward reaching the casual, country-western culture of the cowboy. A lot of people are attracted to such a church, but when the church facility is constructed to resemble a horse arena, the church has locked itself into this approach long-term. Without major expense to alter the building, the church doesn't have a lot of flexibility in its approach to ministry. A church should understand these issues before investing several hundred thousand dollars or more in a specialized or targeted building design.

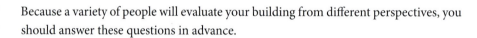

CULTURE AFFECTS FACILITIES. To evaluate what type of building is appropriate for your church, you must first identify whom you are trying to reach. As Ed Stetzer has said, "In many ways, the how of church ministry is determined by the who, when, and where of culture."[1] The culture you are trying to reach, not a preconceived idea of what a church should be, will determine the way you minister, and the same is true of the facility you build to house that ministry. The culture determines the ministry, and the ministry determines the facility.

Because a variety of people will evaluate your building from different perspectives, you should answer these questions in advance.

WHOM HAS GOD SENT US to minister to and/or reach with His message?

WHAT KIND OF MINISTRIES will it take to reach this target group, given their values and approach to life?

HOW DO WE DESIGN (or choose) a facility that will address these ministry needs while maintaining a cost-effective and stewardship-minded approach to the design?

THE CHURCH FACILITY AS A TOOL

The third view of the church facility uses a familiar analogy: a church building is like a tool for your ministry. Tools help us accomplish a task, and they make our work more effective. A good church building does both of these things. Each room should be designed with its purpose or purposes in mind, whether teaching, worshiping, fellowshipping, or doing administration. The room should facilitate the task and make ministry more effective.

A tool amplifies our efforts. Some people in your church may argue that your buildings are just fine as they are and that constructing a new one would be too expensive. They are so used to the existing building and its limitations that they cannot imagine the benefits of a new one.

Have you ever tried to cut wood with a dull axe? Doing ministry in an inadequate facility can be just as frustrating. People are ministering, teaching, and leading with tools that don't fit the needs. Inadequate facilities get in the way of the ministry and generally slow things down. Great effort is being expended with very little result.

If the axe is dull, and one does not sharpen its edge,
then one must exert more strength.

ECCLESIASTES 10:10

With better tools we can get better results. The writer of Ecclesiastes admonishes us to sharpen the tools we have. Your church may need to sharpen the blade for more effective ministry. You may need to invest in getting the tools you have in good shape so that the workers who faithfully give their time and effort can get better results. That's what tools do: they yield better results from the same effort.

You may need to remodel or upgrade your preschool rooms. The youth area may need to be addressed. Does the worship center fit your needs and accommodate the ways the church wants to worship? In fact, you may need to replace that old axe with a modern tool. If your facilities are outdated, you may be surprised to learn how much more effective your church could be with the right tools.

KNOW HOW TO USE THE TOOL. A man went into a store to buy a saw. The bright young salesperson recognized an opportunity, so he went to work selling the man on the benefits of a high-powered chain saw. He promised, "With this baby you can cut three times as much wood in the same time!" The man was sold.

But two days later the man came back into the store dragging the chain saw behind him. He heaved it onto the counter and announced, "I want my money back! This thing is terrible! I worked all day and into the night, and I cut only half as many trees with this worthless thing! It's heavy and slow, and worse than that, it cost 10 times what a normal saw would have cost!"

Perplexed, the salesman looked at the saw and began to apologize, saying something must be wrong with it, that it was guaranteed to work, and that he would get it repaired or replaced if necessary. The salesman examined the shiny new tool and began to examine it to learn what the problem might be. He primed the engine and pulled the starter chord. When the saw roared to life, his surprised customer said, "What's that noise?"

The man had never tapped into the power of the tool. He had missed the whole point.

Once you have a new facility, train your workers in how to use it. Over time they may have adapted to using inadequate tools, and the mere presence of new tools does not guarantee they will be used to their fullest advantage. For this reason, before the new building is complete, take your workers to a seminar or conduct your own training event to teach them the advantages of the new facility and how to care for and use it.

The same can be said of the team designing the building. If they don't understand how the facility will be used, they can miss the whole point. The people who will actually use the building need to be represented during the design process to ensure that the design will facilitate their ministry. Recruit the best people available to serve as consultants to the design team if they cannot be full-time members. For most churches, outside resources can be effective in these roles because the ministry leaders in the church do not necessarily have a strong enough background or wide enough experience to know what innovations could be incorporated. The tool will live up to its potential only if it is designed right and used right.

A CHEAP TOOL MAY MEAN MORE WORK. When purchasing a tool, do you look for the cheapest one or the one that has the features that will help you do the job well? Cost effectiveness is important, but it can be self-defeating if it means getting a tool that is not adequate for the task. A tool that breaks halfway through the job is no bargain. The same is true of your facility. You want a building that will stand up to heavy use for years to come. This applies to the roof, air conditioning, light fixtures, windows, flooring, door hardware, and every other detail. Things that break or wear out prematurely can distract you from the work of ministry. Building a cheap building may cause you to spend too much of your time doing maintenance and not enough doing ministry.

Sometimes it makes sense to get a cheap tool. If you plan to use it only once and throw it away or you don't have a place to store it, you may not want to invest much. But most of the time, church facilities are going to be used for a long time. It is wise to consider the long-term demands when investing in a tool that needs to last 50 years or more.

Things that break or wear out prematurely can distract you from the work of ministry.

Green tools? Considering the long-term return on an investment will reap benefits in the long run. With all the attention given to green building in the past several years, you can obtain a significant savings on utilities with a small investment in more energy-efficient construction of your building. The resulting savings will pay for the initial investment fairly quickly, but do not assume that all such investments are worthwhile. Do your homework before you invest. Your architect should be able to advise you.

Building green is not just about saving on utilities. It is also a matter of stewardship of resources, both economic and natural. In Genesis 1:28 God gave humankind charge of the earth and the animals that inhabited it: "God blessed them, and God said to them, 'Be fruitful, multiply, fill the earth, and subdue it. Rule the fish of the sea, the birds of the sky, and every creature that crawls on the earth.' "

We must be good stewards of all God has entrusted to us. To do less would be to fail in one of the first instructions given to humanity. Be wise and responsible about your use of resources. Your church may not need to achieve a LEED (Leadership in Energy and Environmental Design) certification for its building, but all churches should consider ways to be good stewards of our God-given natural resources.

Have the right tool for the job. Tools are designed to do specific things. That's why screwdrivers, hammers, saws, and knives exist. Multitools have their place, but if you are doing an important job, you want a tool that was designed for the specific task.

Tools also have to be improvised from time to time. For instance, if you wanted to hang a picture on the wall but didn't have a hammer, you might use a rock or a shoe. You could cut a tomato with a pair of scissors, but it would be pretty messy! When you want to do it right, you want the right tool for the job.

A room designed with preschoolers in mind makes teaching the Bible to this age group much more effective. It accommodates their specific needs by providing adequate

---

LEED CERTIFICATION
(Leadership in Energy and Environmental Design)

One of several levels of achievement given by the Green Building Council indicating the use of certain environmentally friendly construction materials and methods. Points are accumulated for the use of design elements that achieve certain benchmarks of sustainable construction practice or performance. The project may achieve a rating from certified to platinum.

room for the furnishings needed, facilities for the workers to wash hands between diaper changes, natural light from windows at a preschooler's level, and so forth. A good worship space accommodates seeing the worship leaders and hearing the music and the spoken word. A recreation building should offer a place to participate in activities in a safe and managed environment. Offices should allow the staff a place to be reasonably comfortable to do their work without constant interruption.

The architect's responsibility is to protect the health, safety, and welfare of the people who use the buildings. This responsibility means designing buildings that at least meet the current minimal standards of practice, usually defined by the latest building codes, and creating an environment that is conducive to ministry in all its forms.

Children need plenty of space for the leaders to set up learning centers and allow movement through the teaching time. Youth need rooms for large and small groups. Adults need a place to study in small groups. Churches need a place to share meals together in fellowship and space to gather before and after services. Parking should be convenient and ample for the attendance. All of these tools can be designed for the job. Some areas, like recreation and worship or fellowship and adult Bible study, can be shared; but others, like preschool space, do not lend themselves to sharing. It's important for church facilities to be the right tools for the job.

DON'T EXPECT THE TOOL TO DO THE JOB FOR YOU! Unfortunately, there is one more similarity between church buildings and tools: the tool will not do the work for you. How many times have you seen this illustrated in your life? You make a trip to the store and buy everything you need for a project, including a new tool. By the time you get home, you're tired and other things come up, so these things sit around for weeks and nothing gets done. The tool doesn't do any good until you take it in hand and use it. Obtaining the raw materials is not the same as having the finished project. The same is true of your church building. The building cannot reach people; but using it to plan, teach, fellowship, worship, minister, and evangelize can get the job done.

ARCHITECTURE

The art and science of designing the built environment. The purpose of our work at LifeWay Architecture is to design structures for people to inhabit and use for Christian ministry.

Never communicate to your church that "all we need to do is build this building, and our church will grow." It may seem that easy, but it's true only if you consistently do the work of the ministry God has called you to. Sometimes constructing a building does nothing for a church but get it deep into debt. Without God's hand on the ministry to make a difference in people's lives, a building can do no good.

The building is only part of the equation. It is just a tool, a means to an end. It is God who blesses our efforts to minister. Buildings are designed to facilitate the work, but it is the work of ministry and the Lord's blessing on it that make a difference in a world that desperately needs the good news of Jesus Christ.

AESTHETICS AND BALANCE. Designing a church building is an opportunity to express beauty and creativity. At the same time, we should try to be good stewards and not spend unnecessarily, knowing the money saved might be spent on missions and ministry. The tension between aesthetics and functionality, beauty and frugality is a constant struggle for a church designer.

Should we design impressive, beautiful, and attention-getting buildings that are culturally relevant as a means to minister to the affluent American culture we are trying to reach? Or should we build simple, unadorned buildings that create a stark contrast to the economy of consumption to demonstrate an alternative ethos? Some would tell you it doesn't have to cost more to design and build a beautiful building. Unfortunately, that is wishful thinking. You may be able to design a building that is attractive and functional, but there are limits to what can be done for little or no cost. You could not build the White House for the same price as your house. There is a big difference, not only in size and shape but also in the materials used, the level of finishes, the details, the workmanship, the lighting, and the aesthetics of the design. Unless you are blessed with gifts of free materials and/or labor, quality design and beauty come at a price. There is no substitute for using quality materials that will last and be energy efficient.

The tension between aesthetics and functionality, beauty and frugality is a constant struggle for a church designer.

FINISHES

Product coatings or materials that make a building's visual impact. Examples are paint, carpet, ceiling tile, and wood stain.

One trick is to sparingly use a few strategically placed design features only in the most visible areas, but even those come at a price. So where is the line for your church? What level of quality can you afford?

The right architect can help you a lot with this balancing act. An architect who can sense your mind-set and ministry goals, knows the right questions to ask, and can adapt his style to your tastes and budget is extremely valuable. It is possible to balance an attractive design and cost-effective, efficient utility as both frugal and wise stewards. Your building should do more than house the ministry; it should creatively express the nature and beauty of God. It may not be easy, but it is possible. Each church has to determine what is appropriate for its calling and community. Each church must examine its priorities and prayerfully determine how to engage the culture through its buildings then respond as God has called it.

Your building should do more than house the ministry; it should creatively express the nature and beauty of God.

What Architectural Style Should Your Building Be?

All churches do not have to look alike. A portico with four massive columns and a stark, white steeple reaching to the sky is not for every church. This style may be your picture of what a church should look like, but that does not mean it is the only way to design a church. The building must be culturally relevant. That means the design depends on the people you are trying to reach.

Who you are as a church is important as well, and this identity should be reflected in the design of the building to some extent; but it is even more important for the structure to respond to the unreached people your ministry is trying to address.

Where Is Your Church?

If you were building a place to meet in central Africa, that building may look like a mud hut. If you were meeting in Japan, it may have grass mats on the floor. In Mexico it would probably be built of concrete block. To build a building that looks like a typical suburban American church in these places would be wrong. The building should be appropriate for the culture it serves, for its mission field.

In suburban America there are a wide variety of cultures, subcultures, and people groups that a church could reach. The shape of your building can be a help or a hindrance to reaching these people, depending on the culture. If you are trying to represent traditional values to the community, you might want the building to look traditional. But if you wanted to attract a disenfranchised and antichurch culture, you would probably be better served to hold church in a storefront or a converted warehouse—a building that says, "We are different." The area where you are ministering has a great bearing on the type of building that is appropriate for your church to build. A thorough knowledge of the people and their culture is essential before designing a building.

Designing Missional Buildings

The geography and demographics of the location where you minister have a great impact on the ministry actions you take to reach people. Also keep in mind that church buildings are for real people, not perfected saints who have grown to full maturity. You are designing facilities to reach lost people and incomplete disciples in a particular location whose culture and perspective shade their view of all they see. Through the filter of their life experiences, they evaluate the church's relevance and determine their own attraction to a place to worship or seek God.

Church facilities are designed in a variety of styles and shapes and qualities to communicate the message in a way that will be heard by different people with a wide range of expectations and tastes. Some people might be less likely to respond if the church building is too opulent and others if it is too plain. Design your building to suit the audience. The audience God has called you to reach is your mission field, and the design of your facilities must address its needs.

As you contemplate the building's impact, the design should focus on the people you are trying to reach, not the people who attend now. That does not mean you can completely ignore the current makeup of the congregation, but maintaining an outward focus will help you keep a sense of perspective about all you are doing.

There is no one right way to build missional facilities. To be missional, by definition, is to be focused and relevant to those you are called to minister to and reach.

Some would say, "But God is our audience. Shouldn't we design to please Him?" That's a good point. God is the audience of One as we worship Him in our hearts. However, if that were the only concern, we would be worshiping in heaven. God has left us here on earth to grow, to reach others, and to lead them to worship Him. So even though God is the object and focus of our worship, some who do not know Him are present in our services too, being influenced and sought as He pursues them in love. We need to make the venue as attractive to them as possible.

God is not impressed with elaborate displays and extravagant furnishings but with the spirit of our hearts and the reflection of His love in our lives. What better way to show these than by designing a building that serves as a magnet to attract lost people to Him?

Why Build?

If you boil it down to its essence, we need church facilities to protect us from the weather so that we can see, hear, and participate in the worship, fellowship, discipleship, missions, and ministry of the church. To accomplish this in an aesthetically appropriate yet cost-effective way is a challenge. But the building should also be more. The facility can be an instrument to advance the church's ministry.

The facility can create a sense of place, a space where something special happens. A well-designed building can facilitate relationships by making people feel safe and comfortable. It can make people feel reverent and create a sense of awe. It can be user-friendly, inviting, and warm. It can say to children that this is a fun place. It can let people know that what goes on here is relevant and meaningful. It can say what happens here is timeless and transcendent.

Your building speaks volumes. The nonverbal communication tells people who you are as a congregation, what you care about, whether you are traditional or contemporary, whether your focus is inward or outward, and how much you care about them.

The facility can create a sense of place, a space where something special happens.

Entering a building project at the wrong time is like going into battle without a weapon.

When Is the Right Time to Build?

A number of factors must be considered before beginning a project. Once it is decided what is needed, the church must determine what resources are available and compare those to the resources required to achieve the goal. Resources include not only finances but also skills and time to carry out a project.

THE NEED

If the facilities the church owns, rents, or borrows no longer meet the needs of its programs and ministries, it may be time to build. Various alternatives should first be considered, such as video venues, the multiple uses of facilities, and so on. Future growth must be anticipated and considered.

To determine what buildings are needed, the church must decide what ministries it is called to do. The church may already have a strong, commonly held calling, or it may take considerable time and outside counsel to clarify these ministry priorities. Once they are clear, the church must determine whether the existing facilities are adequate or what new facilities are required to achieve them before deciding it is time to begin a building program. A good master plan should be created and followed to ensure good stewardship of property and proper sequencing and relationships of the buildings.

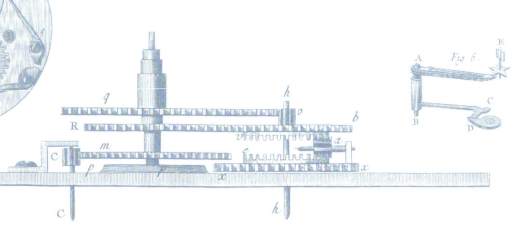

THE FINANCES

Finances for church building projects can come from three basic sources:

CASH IN HAND	PROJECTED FUNDS to be gathered in a capital fund-raising campaign	FUNDS TO BE BORROWED and repaid at a later date

Consult with a knowledgeable financial expert to be sure your estimates of these amounts are realistic. Time to gather financial resources should be considered in scheduling your construction project.

THE SKILLS

Another key resource involves the leadership to move the project forward. You must have the right people available to lead, or the project can be doomed to mediocrity or failure. These leaders will give countless hours in service. If the right leaders cannot give the project the necessary attention due to a lack of conviction or other commitments, the project will lack direction and movement, and church members will lose their confidence in the wisdom of the project.

THE TIME

One of the most important aspects of a successful building project is making a case for why the project is needed, which builds momentum and enthusiasm. Once the project is under way, you do not want to put it on hold because of doubts and questions, losing momentum and effectively having to start the process over again. Jesus referred to it as putting your hand to the plow and looking back (see Luke 9:62).

Find a time when this effort can be given the attention it deserves without conflicting with other activities and commitments. Plan key stages of the project, such as the

CAPITAL FUND-RAISING

The process of soliciting gifts for a specific project consisting of improvements to a physical plant. Most campaigns are modeled after the Together We Build® campaigns introduced in the 1960s. LifeWay Christian Resources still provides this campaign and many other types of fund-raising campaigns for churches.

kickoff of a financial campaign or the presentation of the building plans, at a time when people are available and are not preoccupied with vacations, travel, school, activities, and other potential conflicts. There is no perfect time to launch a project of this magnitude, but the members' availability must be considered.

PEACE WITH GOD

Finally, there is no substitute for the leadership of the Lord. Bathing the building project in prayer and preparing yourself and the congregation for a spiritual battle that can surround a project are key actions. If there is not a sense of peace, assurance that the Lord is leading the effort, and right timing, God may be telling you to wait. Entering a building project at the wrong time is like going into battle without a weapon. It can be costly and disastrous. On the other hand, moving with confidence that the Lord is guiding you to this endeavor provides powerful momentum that can help overcome many obstacles.

As with many things in life, the saying "Timing is everything" could certainly apply to a church building project. If the project is taken on too soon, it will appear that the leadership is pushy and has an agenda the congregation doesn't share. If the project is taken on too late, it could cause the church to miss growth opportunities and perhaps a window of opportunity to build, grow, and reach people.

Waiting for the right time must be balanced with a strong commitment to obedience. If God has made it clear that you need to move, you had better move now! A sense of urgency is important to keep the project from bogging down. All too often, churches wait too long and waste opportunities. Strive for that perfect balance between moving too fast and too slow as God guides you to His timing for your project.

Build Momentum!

Getting a train moving takes a lot of work. Weighing about 1,600 tons, the train starts slowly and gradually increases speed and builds momentum. That is an example of inertia, the resistance to change in an object's motion. Whether it is standing still or moving, an object has a natural tendency to remain in that state. Trying to turn it in a different direction, stop a moving object, or start one moving from a standstill takes energy in order to overcome inertia.

Every church seems to have a certain amount of inertia, a tendency to resist change. Some churches are not moving, and they want to keep it that way.

Other churches have momentum. Momentum is the measure of force of an object in motion (defined as mass times velocity). Once in motion, objects (and churches) tend to keep on moving. The bigger and heavier the object, the more momentum it has, the more inertia it has, and the harder it is to stop.

Once you get 1,600 tons of iron, steel, and freight moving at 50 or 60 miles per hour, almost nothing can stop it.

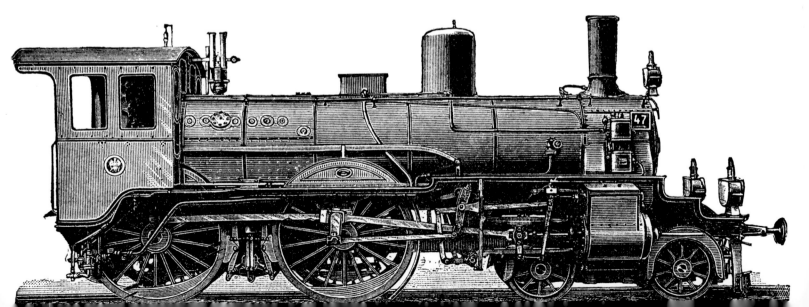

The point of this little physics lesson is that momentum is a desirable trait in a church. It may be hard to get started; but once the church gets moving along a path, it is likely to continue in motion. The church in motion can accomplish much for the kingdom of God. Once movement is started, little things are not as likely to slow it down.

The church in motion can accomplish much for the kingdom of God.

As the project gains momentum, work to maintain it. Lose that momentum, and you can find it very hard to overcome inertia and get it going again. Lots of things can cause a church to lose momentum. For example, a lack of space can cause a loss of energy and eventually bring ministry to a halt. An otherwise healthy, forward-moving church may overcome these obstacles for a while; but if there is not enough momentum to begin with, a little thing can bring the whole machine to a grinding halt.

Once you get 1,600 tons of iron, steel, and freight moving at 50 or 60 miles per hour, almost nothing can stop it. Once the church is on the go and reaching out to people, ministering to the community and seeing the Lord work through them, it is much easier to continue than to start from a standstill. The same is true of your building project. Once it begins to build momentum, don't let it die. Keep stoking the fire to keep it going in order to accomplish your goal.

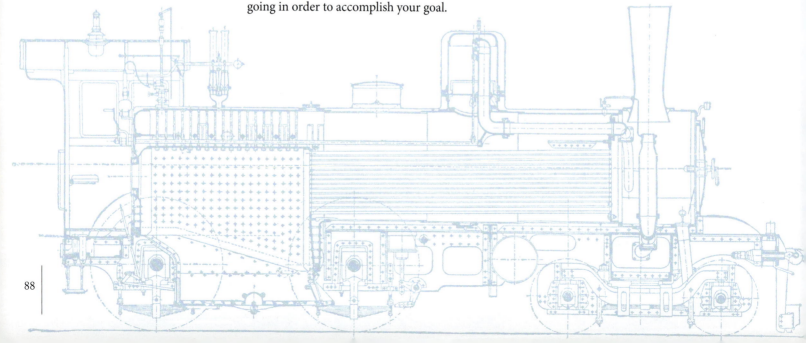

Get on the Same Page

Leaders are responsible primarily for the following two tasks.

PRAYING AND DOING THE RESEARCH AND THE LEGWORK necessary to determine the right course of action for the good of the church and the furtherance of the gospel

GETTING THE CONGREGATION AND THE BUILDING COMMITTEE on the same page and leading them to carry out the project in the right way at the right time

A good place to start is with the church's mission statement or purpose statement. If your church has created this statement, it ought to be the basis on which the project is justified. If done correctly, the statement should have the support of all church leaders. Therefore, when the prospect of building is presented, it should be an expression of the church's mission. If the project is important to the mission of the church, it is worth doing. Building then becomes part of the church's role in fulfilling the Great Commission, and it is your role as a leader to be sure the congregation understands that.

Be careful here. Don't use the Great Commission simply to justify a project. Never use Scripture to justify a move unless it can be applied accurately and you are certain God has called the church to this endeavor.

The church needs to have a vision for its ministry before it tries to design a building. As Davis Byrd, a former director of LifeWay Architecture, says, "If you can't build a paragraph around your ministry-growth strategy, don't build a building around it."[2]

Deal with Expectations

If your church has already decided to build a facility, what did it have in mind when it made that decision? There can be widespread disappointment and/or anger over the results of a building project if the original expectations are not carried out.

On the other hand, simply doing what the congregation expects can be a huge mistake. Your church may miss great opportunities for ministry if the planning process draws only from the church's past experience. Perhaps prayer and discovery efforts reveal that another course of action is needed. It is the leaders' job to broaden the church's view and to expand its knowledge of facilities and ministries so that the church can get the most ministry benefit from the resources invested. The facility may finally look quite different from what was initially envisioned, but that's OK if it is better than the church imagined and if members have been involved in decisions throughout the process.

It is vital that the leaders planning the facility bring the congregation along with them in an educational process that serves as the basis for good decision-making. By educating the congregation about the ministries planned and the facilities designed to support them, the committee can gain the enthusiasm of the entire congregation. More people will support the project, will be willing to fund it, and will be involved in the ministry once the facility is complete. Without such involvement by the congregation, the construction project could be a very lonely experience!

The building committee should have knowledge about the ministries of churches other than their own. Because it is impossible to visit enough different churches to gain a broad perspective, a great start is for leaders to attend a building seminar conducted by LifeWay. This seminar will give you the opportunity to visit with professional church architects and consultants who have worked with a wide variety of ministries across the United States. It is a great way to be exposed to a lot of different ideas and approaches to design and to investigate what might work for your situation.

Your church may miss great opportunities for ministry if the planning process draws only from the church's past experience.

The church's vision should not be what the building looks like or a floor plan. It should be what the church's ministry will become.

Often, well-intentioned people start the planning process with some pretty strange parameters. Sometimes we get calls from churches that have decided to build a 60-by-80-foot metal building. Although the inside is not yet defined, they have already decided on the exterior dimensions and structural frame! This is totally backward. Good design is a function of the needs that will be addressed in the building, not the area on the site where it happens to fit or the price of a pre-engineered building someone is selling. Once the design work is done, that predetermined size might be too wide, too big, or too small. That frame may not be the best way or even the most economical way to span the roof. Some decisions should not be made until program analysis has been done, space needs have been analyzed, and design work has been accomplished.

Occasionally, committees or pastors have a vision of what a building should look like. If it is a vision directly from God, that's one thing; but normally, the vision proves to be more of a dream. Dreaming is an early first step in the creative process, sometimes necessary to get people to think outside what is and what could be. Dreams are good, but they can also be dangerous. We can dream up all kinds of shapes and sizes and ideas that may or may not be what the church really needs. Getting fixated on your dream instead of God's vision is dangerous, especially early in the planning process.

It is particularly dangerous to share your dream with the congregation until it has proved to be a vision from God. Doing so can lock your thinking into one idea too early and tempt you to rationalize it rather than objectively look at the real needs that exist.

The church's vision should not be what the building looks like or a floor plan. It should be what the church's ministry will become. What will the shape of your ministry be in five years? Ten years? Twenty years? What kinds of ministry will you have? Will they be healthy and balanced? Will you reach all ages with a strong Sunday School ministry or home small groups? Will you reach out, minister, grow, and change lives? Will you have a strong missions component? Whom will you reach? Can your church double in size? Explore questions like these to define the future reality for your church.

Clarify the Vision

Acquire background information during the preliminary stage of the building process. Inventory the congregation to see what needs they are aware of, making it clear that this is not a vote. The inventory should accomplish three things.

INVOLVE THE CONGREGATION. They will support what they have helped create.

KNOW WHAT MEMBERS ARE THINKING. Do they think the need is for education, worship, recreation, or something else?

DETERMINE THE TEMPERATURE OF THE CONGREGATION. How excited are they about the project? Do other concerns need to be addressed first?

Once you have determined the pulse of the congregation and its awareness of the needs, you will have some idea of the nature of the task ahead as a project-planning group. If the congregation is not in agreement (which is usually the case), you know you will have to pull them together. If they are in agreement but your analysis shows that the need is not where they think it is, you have to persuade them to do the right thing and be excited about it. That can be a great challenge, but it is critical to the success of the construction project and the ministry of the church.

To clarify the vision for the church requires arriving at a mutual understanding of the future state that the church will strive for. It does not have to come to the pastor in a dream or a flash of lightning. It can be formulated in a team of dedicated believers who share the common spiritual goal of reaching their mission field.

To clarify the vision for the church requires arriving at a mutual understanding of the future state that the church will strive for.

Philippians 4:19 promises that "my God will supply all your needs according to His riches in glory in Christ Jesus." That is a wonderful promise, but it does not say God will provide all your wishes, wants, or dreams. Other verses say that God will fulfill the desires of your heart, but they are qualified with requirements like having integrity, being righteous, and delighting in Him:

The Lord is near all who call out to Him,
all who call out to Him with integrity.
He fulfills the desires of those who fear Him;
He hears their cry for help and saves them.

PSALM 145:18-19

Do not be agitated by evildoers;
do not envy those who do wrong.
For they wither quickly like grass
and wilt like tender green plants.
Trust in the Lord and do what is good;
dwell in the land and live securely.
Take delight in the Lord,
And He will give you your heart's desires.
Commit your way to the Lord;
trust in Him, and He will act.

PSALM 37:1-5

The right question is not "What do you want to build?" but "What do you need to build?"

These verses don't leave room to make a case for constructing a building you don't really need. God's promise was not to give you the desires of your selfish, egotistic, overstimulated appetites but the desires of your heart when it is attuned to Him and when it desires what He desires. James 4:3 warns us, "You ask and don't receive because you ask wrongly, so that you may spend it on your desires for pleasure." So the right question is not "What do you want to build?" but "What do you need to build?"

1. Ed Stetzer and Philip Nation, *Compelled by Love* (Birmingham, AL: New Hope Publishers, 2008), 119.
2. Charles Willis, "Buildings Do Not Cause Growth, Architect Tells Church Leaders" [online], 2001 [cited 15 January 2010]. Available from the Internet: *www.lifeway.com/churcharchitecture.*

CHAPTER 4

Start Where You Are

One of the most important questions is
"What are the church's priorities?"

After setting the general direction for your building project, the planning team can start making more concrete decisions about what type of facility it will be.

Determine Needs

Begin identifying needs in your church by asking: What is the current church attendance in each age group now? How many preschoolers, grade-school children, students, and adults attend? What is the breakdown in each service and in small groups? Will all of these people meet on campus, or will some be housed at an alternative location or time? What other ministries require space? Can some of these ministries share space?

Finally, one of the most important questions is "What are the church's priorities?" This is a million-dollar question because if you answer it right, it just might save you a million dollars by preventing you from constructing the wrong building.

Some churches would answer that question with something like "worship and Sunday School," sometimes adding "and to minister to and reach young families." Yet these same churches would plan to build a family-life center while their Sunday School space was too small, outdated, and out of balance within itself and with the worship space. They were about to make a million-dollar mistake. They had not done their homework to recognize their needs. They might have been struggling for years, even decades, with inadequate space; but until they did an evaluation, they could not see that their inadequate space was holding them back.

To decide what your church needs to build, it will need to go through a process of evaluating the existing facilities and to create a future church profile that the buildings will need to accommodate. You may want to get outside help to evaluate the space in terms of both quantity and quality. LifeWay consultants can give you a comprehensive view of what and how to address your facility needs.

To evaluate your space, you will need to establish criteria to judge its adequacy as a tool for ministry, as a sign to the community, and as a container for future growth. You may want to get someone from outside your church or community to objectively help you with such an evaluation. A general sample is provided in appendix 6, page 220.

Growth Space and Support Space

Three types of space are classified as growth space: worship, education, and parking. These containers define the growth capacity of the church. All of the other space is support space that may enhance the ministry in some way but doesn't define the capacity of the church to grow to the extent that these three key areas do.

The areas you use for these three functions define the growth capacity of the church because they house the core ministries of the church. Other areas, like administration, fellowship, choir rehearsal, recreation, and storage, can make it difficult to do certain things; but they do not limit the numerical growth of the church as a whole.

If you lack administration space, daily life can be very difficult for the staff. If the choir-rehearsal area is too small, the musicians may have to compromise on their preparation. Recreation and fellowship space can enhance the ability to do certain things, but churches do not typically stop growing because they lack these spaces. Even storage space may affect the way you do certain things; but it doesn't limit your ability to grow and reach people in the way a shortage of worship, preschool, or parking space can.

THREE TYPES *of* GROWTH SPACE

1. Worship
2. Education
3. Parking

The space you run out of first will become the limiting factor to the growth of the entire church.

Don't get the idea that you should build only growth space and no support space. Balance is important here too. Build an appropriate amount of each type of space to stay in balance. Choir space could be shared for a time; storage may be minimal for a while; and recreation space may be limited to a fellowship hall, which is also used for Sunday School. Administration may be in temporary quarters for a while to allow you to build the growth space you need; but eventually, resources will allow you to take care of these needs as well. If Great Commission growth is a priority to the church, growth space should be a priority as well.

Balance Is the Key

When any one of the growth areas—worship, education, or parking—reaches its limits, that area tends to slow down or even stop the growth of the entire body. If you have filled the available worship space, it probably would not help to increase the parking or educational space. The reverse is true as well. If you are out of Sunday School space, increasing the capacity for worship or parking without addressing the educational space would not solve the problem.

The space you run out of first will become the limiting factor to the growth of the entire church. The growth will not instantly grind to a halt, and there are certainly times when one area can outgrow the others; but the church will eventually find itself limited in its ministry. For this reason we refer to this phenomenon as constraining the growth of the church. With effort the constraint can be overcome, but eventually the growth will still find a limit. That limit is defined by the space that becomes saturated first.

It is normal for churches to have a higher attendance in worship services, but most want to strive for a good balance. Healthy, balanced churches tend to average around 80 percent of their worship attendance in Sunday School. Whatever your norm is, it will require a balanced capacity to sustain it.

This balance principle even goes one step deeper: the capacity of each age group in Sunday School must be in balance to sustain growth, and the age group that runs out of space first tends to become the limiting factor for the entire organization.

Every church is different; but a healthy, balanced average attendance in a church's educational program typically balances out something like this:

15 PERCENT PRESCHOOL (birth through five years old)

15 PERCENT CHILDREN (grades 1 through 6)

15 PERCENT STUDENTS (7th through 12th grade)

55 PERCENT ADULTS (age 18 and up)

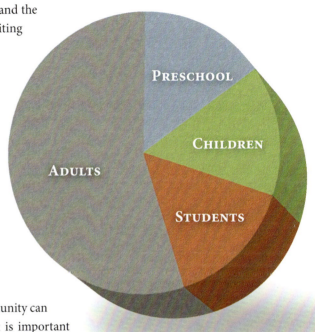

Your church's ministry style and the demographics of the community can have a tremendous bearing on this balance, but in general it is important to strive for balance to ensure the perpetuation and health of the church.

Notice that each of the first three age groups represents six years of life. Therefore, it is logical that each is approximately equal. This does not account for an uneven birth rate or other influences, so you may need to adjust these percentages to fit your local situation; but do not ignore the need for balance.

Also keep in mind that, as the church grows, balance will need to be maintained. On a percentage basis the church should plan for fairly balanced growth distributed among the age groups. Rarely would a church build a student-ministry building and that age group be the only one to grow as a result. All ages tend to grow simultaneously.

All ages tend to grow simultaneously.

If you plan to increase the capacity from 200 to 400 with the distribution percentages listed above, the attendance in the enlarged organization would go from 30 to 60 in each of the first three categories and from 110 to 220 adults in order to stay balanced.

As the church continues to plan for future growth, the need for future space is fairly predictable. The long-range master plan for the growth of the church should always take into account this need for balance and even distribution.

Of course, in some situations there can be other predictable changes in the distribution of the attendance. If, for instance, the church currently averages only 9 percent of its attendance in the preschool area, the limitation in the preschool ministry will have to be addressed in order for the church to grow. In the future the percentage of preschool attendance should begin to rise as compared to the other age groups until a healthy, appropriate balance is reached. This correction may take place over a number of years, or it may be fairly rapid, depending on what is currently impeding the growth and the aggressiveness of the strategies that correct the imbalance.

Be aware that going to a second worship service will rarely help with the growth of the church if the other two elements of educational space and parking are not adequate. All three growth areas must be addressed.

Plan for one car for every two persons you want to attend.

Parking is the most frequently overlooked type of growth space. Many churches were constructed in a time when a large portion of the population walked to church. Research shows that many churches minister in suburban, urban, and even rural communities where the average ratio is about two persons in attendance per car.

Don't let local building officials or an architect mislead you into planning for less parking than you really need by claiming that you need only one space for every four seats in the worship center. That is not a growth-driven regulation, and it is a fraction of the parking you really need. Plan for one car for every two persons you want to attend.

Quantitative Decisions

One of the first things to determine in the planning process is the amount of space you have. Do you have enough space to do the ministry you are called to do?

WORSHIP

First examine the worship space. Count the number of seats, including the choir. We calculate 20 inches per person on pews. Some people are larger than that; but because children will also be present, this is a good average size for figuring the capacity of the room—the number of people it would hold if every seat were full.

Take 80 percent of that number to get what we consider the maximum average attendance the room can sustain. This number represents the number of people your attendance will average once the space has reached saturation. Some days the attendance will be much higher than this number, and other days it will be lower. There may even be days when you have to bring in chairs to have enough seats but other days when the attendance is about half that, such as when people are on vacation or the weather is bad.

When the average attendance in a worship service approaches this maximum-average-attendance number, it is time to do something about your space. You can go to a second service or build; but if nothing is done, attendance will eventually be constrained. You may be able to stretch the envelope for some time; but eventually, it will level off around this number. Certain factors may slightly affect the capacity of the space to sustain this number, including the spacing of the seats, the sight lines, and the number of people in the choir (the 80 percent rule usually assumes a full choir loft). Depending on these factors, the space may reach saturation even sooner.

You may question the validity of this rule of thumb, but our research has shown it to be a good gauge of the worship space. Many churches have been plateaued in their attendance for years, fighting to get beyond a certain level of growth, only to find that when they do the math, they have fluctuated up and down all this time around the 80 percent mark. They were unaware that they were fighting a facilities-related barrier to growth.

Churches that add a second worship hour can usually achieve only about 70 percent of capacity in the second service. Still, a church that is saturated at 80 percent can spend very little or no cash and increase its attendance potential from 80 percent to 150 percent of the capacity of the space. In a room with a capacity of 300, that means the attendance can grow to 450 (150 percent of 300) instead of just 240 (80 percent of 300).

Let's say this 300-seat worship center has 25 pews with 12 persons on each pew. We said 80 percent full would equal 240 people on average. If the choir occupies two pews, that leaves 216 people in 276 seats. But nobody ever likes to sit on the front row, so that eliminates 24 seats, bringing the remaining empty seats in the room to 36. That figure is fewer than two empty seats per pew.

Now a guest walks in with a family of four. Where are they going to sit? The front row? Not if you ever want to see them again! You can see that a room that is 80 percent full feels quite full. If you do not have enough seats together to accommodate families and friends who come together, they will stop coming. Of course, extra room in the worship center will not actually cause growth, but the lack of space can surely restrain it.

EDUCATION

The next area to evaluate is the educational space. Take each class and department room available, measure it, and calculate the capacity using the recommended square footages per person in the classroom space. Measure only open classroom space available for people, not cabinets, closets, and restrooms.

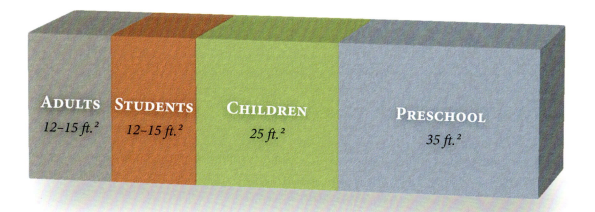

RECOMMENDED SQUARE FOOTAGE PER PERSON

The resulting total will be the capacity for your on-campus small-group ministry. Again, take 80 percent of this number to find the sustainable average attendance in this space. You can compare this figure to the actual average attendance to identify which areas, if any, need additional space. Sometimes you can correct minor deficiencies by moving classes around. Other times there is no alternative but to build additional space.

The 80 percent rule is as valid for educational space as for worship space. On any given Sunday a preschool room may be full, while a senior-adult men's class may have plenty of room. Of course, you can't move preschoolers into the senior-adult men's class. The very next week the preschool class may have room, but the fifth graders are overflowing. You can't move the classes each week to make the most efficient use of the space. Some classes will be less than full, while others are quite full. Eighty percent is what a church can sustain in average attendance.

At the same time, a room that holds 14 children will level off when the attendance reaches 11. An adult class that holds 30 will average only about 24 in attendance over time. Again, 80 percent is the rule for sustainable average attendance.

The 80 percent rule is as valid for educational space as for worship space.

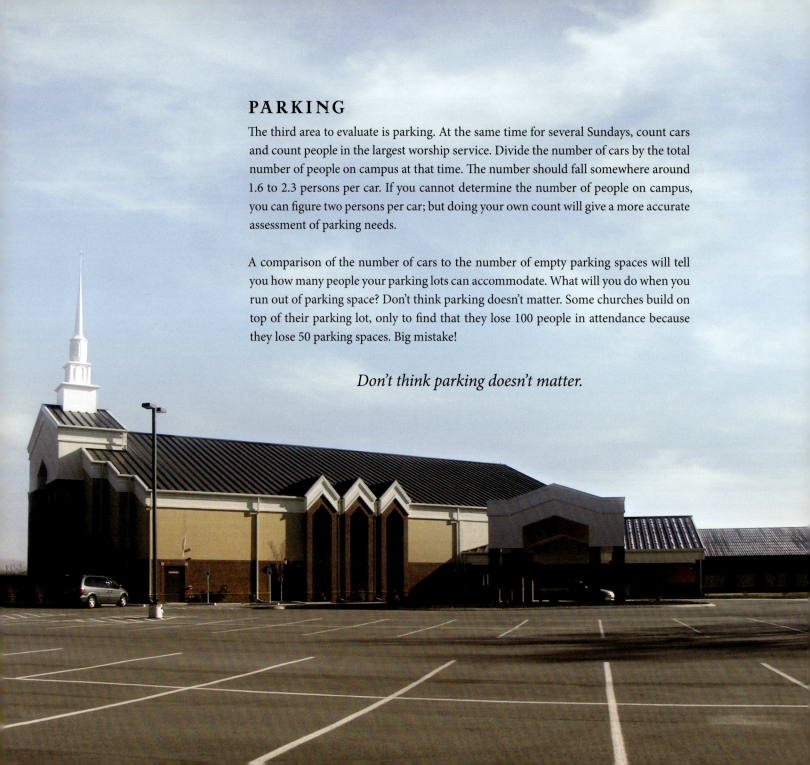

PARKING

The third area to evaluate is parking. At the same time for several Sundays, count cars and count people in the largest worship service. Divide the number of cars by the total number of people on campus at that time. The number should fall somewhere around 1.6 to 2.3 persons per car. If you cannot determine the number of people on campus, you can figure two persons per car; but doing your own count will give a more accurate assessment of parking needs.

A comparison of the number of cars to the number of empty parking spaces will tell you how many people your parking lots can accommodate. What will you do when you run out of parking space? Don't think parking doesn't matter. Some churches build on top of their parking lot, only to find that they lose 100 people in attendance because they lose 50 parking spaces. Big mistake!

Don't think parking doesn't matter.

Don't let the zoning ordinance or a civil engineer suggest that the church doesn't need this much parking. They frequently use outdated data that requires only one space per three or four seats in the worship center. At one space per three seats, you will have too little to fill the building once. Then if the church goes to two services, you will have less than half of what you need. Use the actual parking ratio for your church.

Let's say you are building a 600-seat worship center. An engineer might say you need 200 parking spaces (600÷3). At two persons per car, you will attain an attendance of only 400 people. You could go to two worship services and get 900 people in two services, but you would need 450 parking spaces for that. The city says you need 200, but in reality you will eventually need 450—more than twice their projection! Of course, you will not need all of those the first day; but the master plan should allow for them all.

One final word about room to grow: never say, "The church won't grow until we build this building." It may not be true! God may reveal a plan for multiple services, multiple locations, borrowed space, or another solution that meets the need at least temporarily. Even if it is true that the church will have great difficulty growing, such a statement can become a self-fulfilling prophecy. You may have just given your church the excuse it needs to stop reaching out to new people because you said they can't be reached. Instead ask, "What could our church do if we were not restricted by our current facilities?"

What could your church do if it were not restricted by its current facilities?

Qualitative Decisions

Consider the neighborhood when creating the design parameters for your project.

When you set out to evaluate your space from the perspective of quality, start by examining the homes, offices, and retail space in the area where the people reside whom you are trying to reach. Let this establish a standard of quality. The homes they live in, the offices they work in, and the stores they shop in can communicate a level of expectation they have for their space. If these people are building modest homes, they will be satisfied with modest church facilities. But if they are building large, expensive homes; work in nicely appointed offices; and shop in upscale stores, you will know they will not feel comfortable in plain, dated, aging, or unattractive buildings.

Some church members may say these expectations should not matter, that the people will come if they love the Lord. But these things matter to the people we are trying to reach. Their hearts are not necessarily right with God. They may be lost, and lost people don't yet love the Lord.

To have an opportunity to minister to them, we must understand their culture enough to address their expectations for a built environment. Their culture and expectations may be as foreign to us as ministering in a foreign country, but we must learn to "speak the language" of their culture to be effective.

Church buildings can have a great impact on the ability of your church to fulfill its purpose. Do not underestimate or neglect to plan for this important element in the life of the church. To provide space that serves as an effective tool for ministry, consider both the quantity and the quality of your church facilities.

Preschool Is of Particular Importance

In a large number of churches the greatest need is for a major upgrade of or replacement in the preschool area.

Many churches have fallen behind in keeping up with the quality of the preschool space as standards have risen. Experience shows that an investment in this area could produce the greatest impact of almost anything a church can do.

HIGH EXPECTATIONS

PARENTS WANT THE PRESCHOOL FACILITY TO BE SAFE. Rooms should be designed without hazards and threats to the general safety of the occupants. They need to be on the ground level with adequate exits, fire alarms, and emergency lighting.

PARENTS WANT THE PRESCHOOL AREA TO BE SECURE. Someone off the street should not be able to walk in. Design the area to keep general traffic out; people should not have to go through the preschool wing to get to another part of the building. Toilets that are accessible directly from the preschool rooms will also improve the security since the children will not have to leave the room to go to the restroom. Always include a small view window in preschool classrooms so that the children and workers can be monitored without interrupting the class. Large windows tend to create distractions.

PARENTS WANT THE PRESCHOOL SPACE TO BE SANITARY. Preschool classrooms need a sink in each room so that workers can clean up after spills and can wash hands between diaper changes. It is not acceptable for workers to need to leave the room to wash hands, leaving the children unsupervised or with only one adult.

PRESCHOOLERS ARE VERY REACHABLE

Young families who have new babies often realize they need the support and training the church can provide. At this stage of life, parents gain new perspective and become more open to reordering their values, including making God a higher priority. This can be a great opportunity if the church makes them feel welcome and demonstrates that they share their love and concern for their child.

An investment in the preschool area could produce the greatest impact of almost anything a church can do.

Aesthetic Decisions

Consider the condition of the building, inside and out. The outward appearance of the building and grounds can affect a church's ability to reach people in many ways. A building that appears not to have been updated since the 1950s can be a huge problem to a church that is trying to reach young families today.

For a church that is trying to reinvent itself, a major remodeling or a new building can help create a new image and self-perception for the congregation. It can become a catalyst to launch the church into its future. But it can also act as the proverbial lipstick on a pig. If the change isn't systemic, if the church hasn't really changed from its old ways of doing things, people will quickly discover the reality behind the façade.

On the other hand, for a dynamic, forward-thinking church to continue to meet in a dull and unexciting space would not only be inappropriate but would also have a negative effect on the church's ministry. Jesus said in Mark 2:22, "No one puts new wine into old wineskins. Otherwise, the wine will burst the skins, and the wine is lost as well as the skins. But new wine is for fresh wineskins." In the first century wine was kept in containers made of goatskin. An old wineskin would grow brittle over time, and since wine expands as it ferments, an old wineskin might not be able to accommodate the pressure and could burst. A new wineskin was more flexible, capable of growing and stretching as the wine aged and fermented. Our buildings (as well as our ministries) need to be designed to be flexible and to grow and change with the way we minister. If your existing building can't be adapted to the church's new ways of doing things, it could be hindering your ministry.

The outward appearance of the building and grounds can affect a church's ability to reach people in many ways.

Is it User-Friendly?

Evaluate your existing facility for functionality by asking the following questions.

1. DOES IT MAKE A GOOD FIRST IMPRESSION?

Is it inviting to first-time guests and newcomers to the community?

Does it have ample, convenient parking?

Is it easy to find your way around? Are there functional hallways, gathering places, administrative areas, restrooms, and support spaces?

Is it up-to-date in style and well maintained?

2. IS IT DESIGNED TO SERVE AS A FUNCTIONAL TOOL FOR THE WAY YOU DO MINISTRY?

Does it facilitate the priority activities of the church?

Can it set the appropriate mood for the activity, or are there distractions, poor lighting, or other problems?

Is there room for growth in all age groups and programs?

Is there balanced capacity in all age groups, or is an area being neglected?

Is it safe and secure, minimizing risk and liability?

Is there balanced capacity in all age groups, or is an area being neglected?

3. DOES IT EFFECTIVELY COMMUNICATE WHO YOU ARE AS A CONGREGATION?

Does it show people how much you care about them?

Can people tell that you believe the Lord is important and worthy of your very best?

Alternatives to Building

New construction is not always possible, and even when it is possible, it is not always the right way to address space needs. By going to a second worship service, the church can grow substantially without a major expenditure. Sometimes this avenue addresses the need for growth space. Other times it may be a way to buy time and continue to grow while the church plans and constructs a new building.

Churches of all sizes, with 60 or more in attendance, have seen success with this strategy; but churches with fewer than 300 in attendance tend to have more difficulty with it than larger churches. Up to this size the church is probably very close-knit. Everyone knows everyone, so seeing everyone at the services is important. Beyond this size, the church begins to resemble a lot of little churches. Members can't know and keep up with everyone else, so they don't expect to see them all at every service. When the church reaches this state of growth, multiple services become a more palatable option.

One way to offer multiple services is to use multiple venues. Instead of using the same room two or three times, the church offers services in different locations. The sermon is usually piped into the additional locations via video, but the music is usually live and unique to each venue. The venues may be in the same building or miles apart. This solution requires some rather sophisticated technology to succeed but has grown in popularity over the past few years.

Educational space can be multiplied by expanding the program to extend over two or three hours. This allows classrooms to be used multiple times, except for rooms occupied by preschoolers and younger children, who do not leave to go to worship.

Off-campus space can be used to supplement or replace the need for classrooms. These locations can be homes, offices, hotel meeting rooms, and the like. The advantage is that the church builds less square footage per person reached and therefore can use the

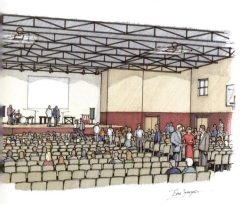

New construction is not always possible, and even when it is possible, it is not always the right way to address space needs.

funds that would have been spent on buildings for other direct ministry. The disadvantage is that churches that utilize facilities off campus usually have a lower percentage of people who attend educational programs, as compared to worship. This option also seems to convey the message that discipleship is not as important as worship and sometimes makes attendance at educational programs more inconvenient, so many people choose to attend only worship.

Determining whether alternatives to construction are feasible will depend on the people you are trying to reach, your church culture, and your approach to ministry.

Churches that utilize facilities off campus usually have a lower percentage of people who attend educational programs, as compared to worship.

Adaptive Reuse of Buildings

There is an encouraging trend among churches to purchase existing buildings and convert them to church use. This approach is nothing new. For years churches have been purchasing adjacent houses and business property for Sunday School or administrative space. The difference is that recently, churches have begun purchasing large, nonadjacent buildings to convert and relocate or to begin a multisite ministry. Sometimes good values are available on shopping centers, big-box stores, or malls that can be converted into viable church buildings. When the cost of land and new construction is too high, adaptive reuse can be a good solution to budget deficiencies.

Consider the following factors before purchasing a building for adaptive reuse.

Before committing to purchase any existing building, perform due-diligence investigation on the property and building, making sure there are no unmanageable environmental contaminants or structural issues that can make the adaptation of the building infeasible. Your architect can help you with this investigation, which will require an investment to get structural and environmental engineers to review and report on the issues. Dry cleaners and service stations are the most common culprits for environmental contamination.

COMPARE THE COST OF PURCHASE AND RENOVATION to the cost of land and new construction. It is not always less expensive to adapt and reuse an existing facility. Making the building accessible to the disabled and suitable for assembly-occupancy fire protection can sometimes be prohibitive.

CONSIDER THE NEIGHBORHOOD, LOCATION, AND ACCESSIBILITY of the existing facility just as you would for a new building. Is this where the building needs to be in order to reach the church's mission field?

CONSIDER PROPERTY ISSUES. Is there room to expand in the future as the church grows? Is there sufficient parking space for the current attendance-to-vehicle ratios with room for growth?

IS THE LONG-TERM COST OF UTILITIES AND MAINTENANCE BEING CONSIDERED? Sometimes an older building has problems in these areas that will make the ongoing costs prohibitive. Solutions like a new roof, additional insulation, or new windows might solve the problem; but they will increase the initial cost of renovation.

WILL THE BUILDING BE ADAPTABLE TO YOUR NEEDS? Is there a place to create a large enough place for worship without too many awkward columns in the way? Are there load-bearing walls that will be expensive to remove? Existing construction drawings of the building would be very helpful for you and your architect to review.

Several churches that chose to convert existing buildings have found tenants to lease part of the building and in this way share the cost with the church. One church purchased a mall and converted part of it for their use and leased the rest to stores. Another church owns a warehouse and leases space to offices and warehouses. These tenants pay the church enough to pay the mortgage, so the church can use the rest of the building for services and ministry for free! Be sure to consult a tax expert in these arrangements to avoid any entanglements or a big tax bill you were not expecting.

The Necessity of Change

Beth Moore has said, "We start dying when we stop changing. If you're still drawing breath, there are still areas where God wants to change you and draw you nearer."[1] Change is always happening around us. How we respond to change is crucial to the vitality and success of our ministries. Certainly, not all change is for the better. Some things were better 20 years ago than they are today. Many people react to the constant change around them by trying to preserve the status quo. If leaders in the church resist change too much, it can be costly to the ministry. If the mission field and culture we are trying to address is constantly changing, we must adapt our methods to continue to address that culture. This can include the buildings we use to reach people. The message stays the same, but the methods change as the mission field changes.

Over the past few years many changes have been incorporated into church design as a response to cultural changes around us. In the United States video technology has advanced so much that churches have adopted video projection as a common method of communicating and reinforcing messages in worship.

A variety of musical instruments have been added to our worship services. Through the middle of the 20th century, only the piano and organ were the norm. Today guitars, horns, percussion, strings, and others instruments are common. It was once rare to see food in the church except for fellowship meals, but now churches regularly serve refreshments like coffee and hot chocolate to adults. Change will always be a part of ministry as long as we are addressing a changing culture.

Some people in your church don't want anything to change! They want to keep things the way they are, with the same staff, the same buildings, and the same songs. However, if we always resist change, we will eventually find ourselves and our churches out of touch with the people we are trying to reach. Our buildings will become relics of the past, and it will become very hard to reach new generations for Christ. As Thom Rainer

We start dying when we stop changing.
BETH MOORE

and Eric Geiger said in their book *Simple Church,* "The majority of churches choose not to change. They would rather die. Tragically, in most churches, the pain of change is greater than the pain of ineffectiveness."[2]

Sometimes buildings become a symbol of change. They become the rallying point around those who do or do not want to change. If some people in your church resist change, they may object to any changes related to building. If they cannot stop a building from getting built, they may attempt to use it as a means of shaping the ministry as it was in the "good ole days." Things like projection screens can become a battleground more for the change they represent than for the impact of the screens themselves.

You cannot stay where you are and go with God.

HENRY BLACKABY

Change is necessary for effective ministry. It should be managed and appropriate, but it is important that we refuse to hold on to old ways at the expense of effective ministry. As Henry Blackaby has said, "You cannot stay where you are and go with God."[3]

Address the Quality Gap

When churches build, they usually do so to address the current level of expectations of the people who are planning the building. The problem comes when the church changes, becoming more affluent or diverse, for example. Building codes become more rigorous, and standards of quality change. Before the church is aware of it, the buildings that met expectations in the 1970s no longer meet the expectations of the people they are trying to reach today. Accessibility for the disabled is an expectation today that older buildings, some erected as recently as the early 1990s, do not address. To stay relevant and minister more effectively, these buildings need to be updated.

Expectations for space have also changed. In midcentury America an 1,800-square-foot home was considered large. Now it is considered modest, and houses in excess of 3,000 square feet are common. Similarly, people today expect public buildings like church facilities to be spacious as well.

Prior to the 1920s, indoor plumbing was not even common in churches. Now we expect restrooms to be sanitized; furnished with ceramic tile floors, plastic laminate, or enamel steel toilet partitions; multiple stalls; good lighting; and so on.

When our facilities do not match the expectations of the people we are trying to reach, there is a quality gap. Over time facilities deteriorate. Carpet wears out, colors go out of style, and walls get scratched. At the same time, society's expectations go up: the building code demands more exits, people want more space, and the disabled want accessibility. An ever-widening gap between the expectations of our mission field and our church facilities can cause a crisis of relevancy. The people we want to reach look at our facilities and conclude that we are out of touch and irrelevant to their lives.

The need for long-term effectiveness demands that we evaluate the expectations of the people we are trying to reach and exceed them. Both parts of this statement are important. First and most importantly, we are designing the building to please the people who do not yet attend there. Our focus must be on the people we are trying to reach. If we design simply to please the current membership, we can miss the boat!

Look at the changing culture around your church. Is it in transition? Is it becoming more affluent? Is the educational level rising? Are there more professionals and fewer blue-collar workers or farmers? Identify the people you are trying to reach for the future. They should determine the way your next building is designed. The building you are planning today will most likely still be in place in ministry 20, 40, or even 50 years from now. Although only God can know that, think carefully about the way you do construction so that you are not knowingly building in obsolescence.

The second key is not just to meet expectations but to exceed them. If we build to meet only current expectations, we will likely find ourselves falling behind very quickly as those expectations change. Expectations very rarely go down. Even in the Great Depression years, expectations continued to rise as building technology improved.

Good-quality construction means many things, including quality finishes that can be cleaned and maintained, good insulation to avoid high utility usage, efficient heat and air-conditioning systems that will keep up with the demand and last for many years, quality pavement, durable flooring, commercial-grade fixtures, and on and on.

Some of these features are more important than others. Carpet can be changed in a few years, but changing a corridor that is too narrow or replacing ductwork can be prohibitive. If there are cost constraints, we must carefully choose where to compromise and where to invest. Some things can be added as funds become available, while others must be done right from the start.

Considering the needs of your target ministry field and making efforts to exceed their expectations will help ensure that your church facility remains relevant and serviceable far into the future.

Provide Room to Grow

To allow for growth, your existing worship, education, and parking should exceed your current attendance by a significant amount. We recommend at least 50 percent, even more in fast-growing situations. If you don't have this minimal growth space, your church will have to address this need. The goal of your church is to reach out and grow.

Ask yourself questions like:

WHAT IF THE MINISTRY is successful and increases the number of prospects and new members who come into the church?

CAN THE EXISTING FACILITIES handle the additional attendance you are trying to create?

The facility you build now may be all you can do for a while. Don't deplete all of your financial resources to build recreation space and then realize that the church also needs space for worship, education, or parking.

Keep in mind that a building project will take two to three years to complete; then it may take additional time to finish paying for it. You can see it may take several years to start the planning and building process for another phase of worship or educational space and even longer to occupy it. Generally speaking, it typically takes at least six years between building phases, usually longer, so your educational and worship space will need to accommodate any growth experienced for at least that interval.

Finally, consider the balance of space throughout your facilities. All of the various types of space need to balance to allow for growth. For instance, building additional youth space will not typically satisfy the needs of preschoolers. Plan for growth to happen in all age groups and accommodate them with appropriate space to meet their needs. It is imperative to consider this balance when evaluating your church's capacity for growth that may occur over the next several years.

Have Clearly Defined Priorities

Before spending a large portion of the church's income on a particular ministry or on a building, be certain the pastor, staff, and congregation have a strong sense of calling to this ministry strategy.

The church, collectively and individually, should understand its mission and strategies to fulfill that mission. The reality is that when resources are limited, certain programs must take a backseat to others. For instance, recreation should never become the primary purpose of the church, but its position on your priority list will determine the amount of your resources that are appropriate for you to allocate to this ministry.

When resources are limited, certain programs must take a backseat to others.

The object here is to avoid the "tail wagging the dog" syndrome. When an inappropriately large amount of a church's resources are put into any ministry, other aspects of the ministry tend to suffer. The highest priorities are typically the core areas of worship, Sunday School, and missions. After these are funded sufficiently, a number of other programs begin to step in and compete for resources. Very careful decision making and planning should guide which program gets how much funding, based on strategic plans for the overall ministry of the church, not based on who speaks the loudest at meetings. Start by ranking items into three major categories

ESSENTIAL. Items that are essential to the existence and viability of the church should be classified as core needs for the building project. Include only the items that must be included to accomplish the most basic ministries of the church. This may leave out some items that are expected to be in the project, however this category is not for expectations but core needs. It should be a very short list of only a few very important areas that are essential for the church to fulfill its purpose.

IMPORTANT. The next tier of needs includes other items that are important, successful, or widely anticipated but are not deemed to be core programs or ministries. These areas might be considered optional for a devoted believer's participation.

WELCOME. The final category includes items that would be a welcome addition to the church's ministry, but their absence would not impact the health or growth of the church and would be felt by relatively few members. Some items may belong here even if a highly vocal group champions them.

Do not try to discuss the relative merits of items within a category at this time. Simply place each item in one of the three categories. Most of these will fall into place quite easily by consensus. A few items may require a vote to determine their placement. If a number of people have strong feelings about both sides of an item in question, place it in the higher category for now.

At this point you may wish to involve an outside consultant to help your church evaluate your needs and make recommendations about what kind of space would yield the greatest benefits for your ministry. He or she may see needs you hadn't considered and priorities you hadn't realized.

Next go back to each category, starting with the third one, and rank the items within that category from most to least important. Give proponents an opportunity to voice their opinions about a need. Encourage people not to despair if they see their priority at the bottom of the list. Often these items still find their way into the building, especially if they are low-cost, high-yield features that can be paired or share space with a higher-priority item.

You may rank priorities through discussion or by having each member vote his or her opinion, ranking the items from 1 to 10. Then compile a list, using a point system. Give each item that received a vote 10 points for the first priority, 9 points for a second-place vote, and so on.

Starting with the third and least critical group may help team members grow accustomed to working with one another, understand the process of negotiating, and learn how to make group decisions before they deal with the higher-priority items that are more critical to the success of the church.

Proceed to the second, then to the top category of items, using the same evaluation and ranking process. This step should produce a prioritized list of your church's needs to give to your architect.

Qualifications for the Planning Team

The planning team that puts together a building project should consist of some of the wisest people in the church. Consider these qualifications for members of the team.

THE MOST IMPORTANT QUALIFICATION IS TO BE A COMMITTED DISCIPLE. These leaders should be strongly driven by a love for Jesus and His bride, the church. You can hire knowledgeable church consultants, designers, stewardship consultants, contractors, and lawyers; but you can't hire someone to have a passion for your church's mission.

THE LEADERS ON THIS TEAM NEED TO BE FAMILIAR WITH YOUR CHURCH and how it uses its space, particularly the part of the space with which you are dealing. They need to be able to tell the architect what works and what doesn't. No one is better suited for this role than the workers who are now using the space.

THE TEAM NEEDS TO BE COMMITTED TO SEEING THE PROJECT THROUGH. From its infancy to completion, more and more information must be exchanged among all of the people involved. Anytime a team member has to be replaced, time is lost and information is missing because each new person has to be brought up to speed; rarely will the person ever get caught up. Big mistakes can be made simply because someone left and the new person acted on incomplete information.

HAVING VARIETY IN AGE, ECONOMIC LEVEL, GENDER, AND LENGTH OF CHURCH MEMBERSHIP on the team brings representation from various points of view into the conversation. The greater the variety, the more likely church members will feel they have a voice on the committee, and they might be more likely to listen to the recommendations of team members. If longtime members are the only ones allowed to have input, the discussion will lack insight that could be offered from a fresh perspective.

QUALIFICATIONS
for the PLANNING TEAM

1. Disciple
2. Familiarity
3. Commitment
4. Variety
5. Availability
6. Respect
7. Decisive

AVAILABILITY IS AN IMPORTANT QUALIFICATION because the entire team needs to be present for most meetings. Missed meetings can cause information lapses that can lead to misunderstandings, hurt feelings, wrong assumptions, inappropriate decisions, and compromise in the resulting tool for ministry. Team members should not be so busy that they cannot attend the meetings and do the work.

THE TEAM NEEDS RESPECTED LEADERS. Enlist people whom others will look up to and will listen to when they share recommendations that have been developed from hours of study and work.

TEAM MEMBERS NEED TO BE THE BEST DECISION MAKERS IN THE CHURCH. They need to have the wisdom and strength of will to take decisive, thoughtful action. The people on this team need to be able to quickly analyze information; evaluate it; and make rational, appropriate decisions.

Notice some of the qualities that are not mentioned. You don't need to put contractors, plumbers, and electricians on the team just because they know something about construction. They can be a distraction if they are concerned about that aspect of the design and do not look at the big picture. However, if they have the preceding qualities in addition to their specialized knowledge, they can be great assets to the team.

Communicate About the Project

The way the building project is presented to the congregation makes a big difference in the enthusiasm and momentum generated. The perception of the persons receiving the message is important. If they get only a brief, cursory review of the high points, they will not likely be very enthusiastic about the construction project or about giving to make it happen. If the team presenting the proposals seems divided or weak in their enthusiasm, the congregation will respond accordingly.

Open communication is a great way to create and maintain interest in the project.

When someone yells across the house, "Supper's ready!" family members will probably think the meal is going to be fairly ordinary, nothing to get excited about. But say, "Dinner is served" in a dignified tone, and a different expectation is generated. That's the kind of expectation you want to create when communicating to the congregation about the building project. You want people to understand that a lot of work has gone into planning and preparation. It is imperative that they understand things that it may have taken you months to figure out. Take your time to do it right. If they see your enthusiasm, they will be more likely to follow your leadership.

Be careful, however, because enthusiasm can also be misinterpreted as impatience. Church members need to know that you are excited but that you are willing to discuss the merits of the path the committee has chosen. They need to know that you have done your homework and that there is urgency about the project, but they should not feel that you are trying to force your plans on them.

Open communication creates and maintains interest and builds confidence in the congregation. Members who feel informed and up-to-date—even if there is bad news—are in a better position to support the project with their prayers as well as their finances.

COMMUNICATION TIPS

Make building needs an item of prayer long before any other action is taken. If you are not praying about it, how important can it be?

Give regular updates to the congregation through newsletters, the church's Web site, verbal reports, and other channels. Remember that in any given worship service, only about one-half to two-thirds of the congregation is present, so an announcement will miss a large portion of the congregation, even if they are listening!

Select a spokesperson for the building team who has excellent public-speaking skills and believes in the project.

Emphasize the process, not just the end product, as the team works toward its goals and does its work. It is more important that you heard input from all department heads and met twice with the architect than, for example, that the building will have 12 rooms and 21,000 square feet.

Communicate at various levels: technical and logical for those so oriented and more perceptual and sensory oriented for the others in the congregation. Most will not be technically inclined, so keep in mind that they will be more concerned with financing and aesthetics than structural systems and heating, ventilating, and air-conditioning (HVAC) design.

Early in the process give opportunities for feedback and input from the congregation to build a sense of ownership and shared responsibility.

INCLUDE INFORMATION ABOUT GROWTH TRENDS AND FUTURE NEEDS that are being addressed to create and maintain a vision for the future.

INCLUDE EVERY AGE AND INTEREST GROUP IN THE CHURCH in both planning and communicating the project. People will listen and respond better when they hear from a trusted peer rather than someone they don't know.

MATCH THE LEVEL OF INFORMATION WITH THE STAGE OF DESIGN. Don't jump ahead and discuss details that cannot be determined until the big picture is finalized.

PROVIDE TOOLS such as timelines, graphs, square-foot analyses, artist's renderings, models, and other visuals to help visually oriented members understand the project.

GIVE BOTH PUBLIC AND PRIVATE, LARGE-GROUP AND SMALL-GROUP OPPORTUNITIES to ask questions about the project. Some people are too shy to ask in a large group but still need an opportunity to have this interaction.

BE POSITIVE. Let the people know that obstacles will arise; but they will be addressed, and you will move on. When obstacles come, you can confidently say they were expected, and you are on top of the situation. Convey your assurance that whatever the outcome, God will use it for His purpose.

USE YOUR CAPITAL-CAMPAIGN CONSULTANT to help with communications. His or her expertise and experience can help greatly in communicating details of the project.

USE HIGH-QUALITY PRINT AND MEDIA-PRODUCTION SERVICES to communicate the nonverbal message that this project is important. Some capital-campaign companies offer these services, providing professional-looking materials at a reasonable cost.

ANTICIPATE HARD QUESTIONS and put answers in writing.

EMPHASIZE THE MOST SELLABLE ELEMENTS. For example, worship is more sellable to a congregation than storage space.

DISCUSS CONTINGENCY PLANS that are in place in the event of budget problems.

NEVER PRESENT MORE THAN ONE OPTION AND LET THE CONGREGATION CHOOSE. This creates a win/lose scenario. Those who voted for the option(s) that didn't win may feel alienated and remove themselves from the process. Always come with a strong recommendation that the committee has decided to present.

Always come with a strong recommendation that the committee has decided to present.

Unity is a great thing for a church, but it should never divert the church from its purpose.

Deal with Negativity

No matter how effective your presentation to the congregation is, some members will react negatively. You cannot change that. But you can reduce negative responses by presenting your recommendations in such a way that members have time to process what they hear and don't feel backed into a corner. If people are forced to take sides too early in the conversation, it becomes a win/lose situation.

Give members an opportunity to think about the proposal. Some people like to mull things over. If you try to rush them, right or wrong, you will have made an enemy. It may be that people who are saying no to your idea really mean "Not yes yet." Given time, they might warm up to the idea and become strong supporters. But if they are pushed into making a hasty decision, they will vote against it every time.

However, you don't need to give the church 10 years to think about a plan. One church we consulted with 11 years ago is still trying to win over a few reluctant members. Sometimes a church must move on without unanimity. Unity is a great thing for a church, but it should never divert the church from its purpose. All too often we see churches in a stalemate because they will not move forward without a 95 percent vote. Even a 60 percent vote can be difficult to obtain, but that is not always bad. It demonstrates that the church has a variety of maturity, interests, and spiritual motivation.

Win Support

You would never give the least spiritually mature members of the church control over something as important as spending a million dollars of the Lord's money. But in effect, that is what you do if you say the project can't go forward without a high-percentage approval. If the church insists that 80 percent of members must approve the project, that means only about 20 percent of the most disagreeable, selfish, immature, misguided, or fearful members are needed to stop the church from moving forward.

Certainly you should try to get the highest possible level of support for the project, but letting a few unenthusiastic church members hold it hostage is wrong. It takes honesty and wisdom to decide when it is time to move on with the project without a certain portion of the congregation on board, but sometimes it is necessary.

The number of people who oppose the project is one issue. Who those people are is another. If they are engaged, spiritually mature believers with strong reservations, their hesitancy should give you pause. The amount of money they give is not the point. The fact that they are not ready to join this effort could indicate that God is saying you should wait. These members could also be waiting to see how strongly you believe in the project. In this case they are seeking strong direction from the project leaders.

Also consider how strongly these members oppose the plans. If they are neutral rather than actively antagonistic, this neutralism is very different from steadfast opposition. Sometimes people will attack you rather than the project. Sometimes they oppose any change. The task of the leaders is to determine whether the opposition has any validity and to lead by correcting your path or by finding a way to continue the project in spite of dissent.

If your church votes as a congregation on such matters, try beforehand to get a good idea of the likely outcome of the vote. You don't want the project to come up for a vote just to get turned down. This failure would be a huge emotional setback for the congregation and reduces momentum. Instead, informally poll the congregation by going to Sunday School classes or small groups and asking them how they are leaning. Find out what the objections might be and address them so that all can hear and understand. If one person objects to a certain aspect of the project, others probably agree but are not speaking up.

Once you have identified the objections, begin to address them. Speak with the objectors away from their peers and privately ask what you can do to answer their questions. Sometimes you or they just misunderstand the situation, and clear communication will resolve their objections. You can win over a lot of people if you talk with key leaders who will become supporters of the project and will influence others.

Enlist leaders who initially opposed the project to give testimonies in worship services about why they thought it was wrong but now think it is the right thing to do. If they are not good public speakers, publish their written testimonies in the church bulletin or newsletter. Do everything you can to build your case in the minds of the people.

When to Confront

Sometimes it helps to speak with the opposition one-on-one. Face-to-face you can sometimes get to the core of the reasons for opposing the project and gain insight for dealing with them. You may alleviate fears and win over the opponents, or you may succeed in getting them to stop voicing their objections for the sake of the church. Even if there is no improvement, you will have made a good-faith effort. Be careful, however, not to give them the impression that they have power over the project. Do not let them think they can call the shots or have veto power, but state that their comments will be discussed and considered at the committee level as long as they are willing to get on board once the decision is made to proceed. Heed Jesus' instructions for winning a brother: "If your brother sins against you, go and rebuke him in private. If he listens to you, you have won your brother" (Matt. 18:15).

Most of all, pray before deciding to confront those who oppose the project. Attempting to convince them may be a waste of time, or it may be wise. If you win them, they can be great assets; if you don't, they can cause greater problems. Prayer and discernment will help you know what to do: "If any of you lacks wisdom, he should ask God, who gives to all generously and without criticizing, and it will be given to him" (Jas. 1:5).

If any of you lacks wisdom, he should ask God, who gives to all generously and without criticizing, and it will be given to him.

JAMES 1:5

134

Take Time to Ensure Success

Something as major as a church building program is too important to throw out for open debate and then vote on in the same meeting. Instead, start preparing the congregation early. Even if you have no significant opposition, you need to build a case for the project and give members a few weeks or longer to process the information, ask questions, and grow accustomed to your ideas.

As you explore needs, learn about possibilities, develop solutions, and finally make a recommendation to the church, you will learn a great deal. You may end up recommending a solution that would have surprised you at the outset of the process. Keep that in mind as you communicate the project to the rest of the congregation. The average church member cannot fully comprehend in a single meeting what may have taken months for you to process and adopt as the right solution.

In fact, it may take several exposures to the plans for the building project before its wisdom begins to sink in. Have patience and respond in love to church members' questions. Be honest and truthful about all aspects of your presentation of the project. If you do not know some of the details, do not make something up; say you do not know. Do the necessary research and report on it later.

Start preparing the congregation early.

The Emotional Side of Building

The decision to build a church facility is almost always fraught with emotions. One of the most common mistakes leaders make when considering building or relocating is to underestimate the emotions involved in the decision. Even those who recognize the effect of these negative emotions do not always know how to deal with them. If underestimated or not dealt with properly, feelings like anger, fear, resentment, regret, and loyalty can create so much strife that the church ceases to be effective in ministry and outreach. In this unfortunate case the church may no longer have a need to build.

Why does a building project elicit strong emotions? Because it represents change, and change can be frightening. It can mean a loss of power for some who have exercised a certain amount of control in the church. It can symbolize a transition from being a small family church to a larger one. A church changes as it grows, and not all members will be glad for that. However, that is no reason to stop growing. It would be unhealthy to try to stop the growth process when babies begin to crawl or when teens begin to date. As with children, there comes a time to let the congregation grow out of some things and become something new.

It is possible to have a positive experience while building or relocating a congregation. For that to happen, leaders need to prepare for members' emotional responses.

First recognize that the intellectual decision to build is only half of the equation. Expect strong emotional responses from some church members, especially if you plan to tear down an old building or relocate. For this reason be absolutely sure building is the right thing to do before the church goes through the potentially traumatic process of funding and planning a building.

For some members, it doesn't matter why the church is considering the building project; their feelings still make it difficult. No matter how logical and spiritually well founded the decision may be, a number of emotionally wounded members are deeply disturbed by the decision. Some argue. Some fight. Others silently stew about it. Even if they are silent, the feelings don't go away quickly. Often at least one person in a congregation is quite verbal in expressing his or her emotions.

Emotional responses are evident when members begin to tell sentimental stories about the effort and sacrifice that went into constructing the existing structures. They will sometimes say irrational things like "I'm not leaving" or make rash statements about tearing down an existing building "over my dead body." Comments like these are usually few enough in number to ignore, but don't. Instead, be loving and kind to these members as they deal with their feelings.

Dealing with emotional reactions begins before the decision to build has been made. During the discussion phase you are simply asking members to be open to the possibility that God is leading the church to build. At this stage people may feel that if they are open to the project, they are inviting it to happen. They may fear that if they don't fight it, it will surely happen. Be careful not to stir up negative emotions that could cloud the decision-making process. Timing can be very important. Don't get in too much of a hurry. Be careful not to communicate that the decision is already made and that you are not open to opposing ideas about the construction project.

Understand that dealing with emotional arguments as if they were logical arguments about the merits of the decision-making process will not work. Acknowledge that members' feelings of reluctance are valid. Publicly recognize that the existing facility is a symbol of ministry accomplished by members who have worked hard for many years. Recount the history of wonderful ministry that took place in an old church building.

Be loving and kind to members as they deal with their feelings.

Point out that it is OK to have feelings of reluctance, but those feelings are not reasons to ignore God's calling and direction for the church. Help members separate their feelings from the greater mission of the church. Both can be valid. In spite of how members feel, the church must choose to use its God-given abilities to research, evaluate, and discover ways to minister more effectively. Then weigh this endeavor against the intangibles of emotional and personal costs. Ultimately, whether the decision is to build or not, it needs to be the result of God's leading. Encourage members to set aside personal feelings for the greater good of the mission and calling of the church.

Once the decision has been made to build or relocate, help those who opposed the idea to be positive about the future at the same time they deal with their feelings. Some will feel that the church is abandoning its great past. Assure them that past efforts will not be forgotten and enlist them to make sure this doesn't happen. Here are some ways to convert emotional energy into positive outlets that document the past.

CREATE A PHOTOGRAPHIC RECORD of the old facility.

PUT TOGETHER A SCRAPBOOK of memorabilia from the old building.

RECORD STORIES of events that occurred in the old building.

SELECT A WINDOW OR ANOTHER ARCHITECTURAL ELEMENT that can be preserved and incorporated in the design of the new building.

Be careful not to preserve so much from the previous building that you encumber the design of the new building with relics. Space may be limited, and moving certain elements could be expensive. It would be premature to guarantee a prominent location for a display, but a key element might be selected in case there is an appropriate place in the new building.

For some church members, dealing with razing an old building or relocating to a new campus will be like going through a grieving process, as if they were losing a loved one. And in a way, they are. Allow them to grieve. That's OK. No amount of reasoning will ease the pain for some. When dealing with emotional church members, use the same tact and sensitivity you would with a grieving family member who was dealing with a loss. Carefully move the process forward and help them focus on the future while not forgetting the past. Life goes on, and they may need time to accept that.

Try to find healthy ways for these members to vent their feelings without infecting or crippling the rest of the congregation that is ready to move forward. Allow them to talk about what has gone on in this building, their memories, and what they will miss. In an appropriate setting you might even want to invite testimonies about ways the Lord has impacted lives in the previous building. Offer members opportunities to express their favorite memories. Then ask, "What do you look forward to in the new building?" Transition the focus to the mission of the church and what you can do in this new facility that you could not do in the old one—new ministries, new souls won, and lives changed. Ideally, you can allow grieving members to express fond feelings for the old building without having negative feelings toward the new one.

Your responsibility as a leader is to help the congregation move in the right direction, not just take the path of least resistance. As you lead, let the church sense your heart to reach new people and your care for existing church members' feelings as well. Pray that there will be few if any negative feelings about the construction project and for a smooth transition to a bright new future for your church.

Preserve a part of the old building as a part of the new.

Lead with Authority

When the church approves the construction project, be sure to get the authorization necessary to make plans proceed. The team needs to be empowered to weigh decisions and make good choices on behalf of the church for most day-to-day decisions during the building process. You should not need to go back to the congregation for approving the contracts with the architect and engineer, applying for a permit, changing the floor plan, and so on. Throughout the project the team should report to the congregation on the progress being made, but you should not be required to get permission for every decision that is made. If the congregation has to approve every detail, your project will take much too long and is likely to result in numerous battles. Each battle risks more unnecessary conflict in the congregation.

For a church to grow and flourish, leaders must be allowed to act on new ideas.

For instance, whom you interviewed, the fees, how the candidates interacted with your team, and many other factors enter into the decision to contract with a particular firm. It is impossible to bring all of that information to the entire congregation each time a decision needs to be made. The building team, not the congregation, is in the best position to make these decisions. Making good decisions and moving the project forward are what the building team was appointed to do.

The ability to obtain this kind of authorization depends on the history of the church and the trust developed by the building team and the church staff. In some churches every decision to spend more than a certain amount of money is required to be taken before the congregation for approval. This kind of organizational paralysis can keep the church small and ineffective. For a church to grow and flourish, leaders must be allowed to act on new ideas.

The way decision making takes place in the church also affects the church's ability to move forward. Sometimes restrictions that have been placed on decision making limit the church's growth to a certain level. This result may not be intentional, but that is the outcome. Sadly, in other cases a lack of growth is the objective. Certain members do not want the church to grow because they do not want to let go of control.

Allowing the team to function with authority frees it to make decisions in a timely manner and with its best judgment, not what it thinks it can "sell" to the congregation. This authority needs to be balanced with a measure of accountability. Any small team of church members should not be given a blank check to do as they wish.

The building team should seek input and regularly report to the congregation the actions it has taken, the problems it has encountered, and the progress it has made. This kind of open accountability will help build confidence in the process and allow the team to continue functioning freely.

In some churches this freedom will have to be earned. Due to an unfortunate past event, church members lack the trust to allow the team to function this way. Perhaps over time trust can be earned. A series of open reports can give the congregation confidence that the team understands its accountability to the church and to God.

Allowing the team to function with authority frees it to make decisions in a timely manner and with its best judgment.

1. Polly House, "Beth Moore Tells Women to Leave Egypt and Head Toward Canaan" [online, cited 15 January 2010]. Available from the Internet: *www.lifeway.com.*
2. Thom S. Rainer and Eric Geiger, *Simple Church* (Nashville: Broadman and Holman Publishers, 2006), 229.
3. Henry and Richard Blackaby and Claude King, *Experiencing God* (Nashville: LifeWay Press, 1990), 156.

CHAPTER 5

Prepare to Build

Your building design should fit into the
big picture of the church's mission.

Establish a Preliminary Project Budget

Let's begin with some rules of thumb to gain perspective on the budget for a church building project. Most churches can afford to invest up to four or five times their annual undesignated income, that is, their regular budget offering for the year, not counting special missions offerings or capital campaigns. Each church is different, so this general guideline is not a guarantee that your church will be able to invest this much; but it is a reasonably accurate estimate for defining the scope of the project early in the process. We will introduce some other tools that will give you a more precise estimate of how much building your church can afford.

First let's consider where the money comes from. The three primary funding sources for church projects are cash on hand, capital fund-raising, and borrowing.

CASH

The first source of funding seems easy enough to evaluate. How much money does the church have on hand that can be spent on the building? Unfortunately, determining this figure is not always as easy as it sounds. Designated funds in many churches are available only if they build a certain thing, like a new sanctuary, so if the need is for a new preschool building, those funds are not available.

Of course, such limitations on funds given should be discouraged since they are simply attempts to control the decision-making in the church and can lead to inappropriate efforts to capture the funds. A gift is a gift, and the recipient of the gift, not the giver, should decide how it should be used. If the donor does not relinquish control, it is not really a gift but coercion. IRS rules are very specific about this point, so be sure your donors understand the limitations they have over the use of money once it is given.

CAPITAL FUND-RAISING

The second source of funding is through a capital campaign. This campaign is usually a well-organized program that informs the congregation of the nature of the need, the type of project planned, and the opportunities for giving. When done correctly, capital fund-raising can provide an excellent opportunity to teach stewardship principles and to challenge members to think differently about their possessions. Through such a campaign many families understand and experience God's provision for the first time. The funds that result from the program generally come in over a three year period. The cash flow from the program must be timed so that the need to borrow does not exceed the church's capacity (or targeted limit) at any given time in the process.

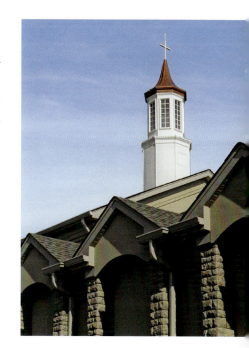

Obviously, the more your church can raise in cash from a campaign like this, the less you will have to borrow; therefore, capital fund-raising is one of the most important parts of the entire building process. Failure to reach the full potential of the church's giving can cost tens of thousands of dollars. For this reason we strongly recommend that the church get a professional consultant to assist with the campaign. You cannot afford to risk 25 to 50 percent of the project's budget because the church wanted to save the expense of an outside consultant. The best results come in churches that use outside professional consultants to help them do a first-class job of making the campaign a scriptural, spiritually focused event, such as the Beyond Measure® program. Contact LifeWay's Stewardship Department at (800) 251-4220 to find a consultant who can assist with a fund-raising campaign in your church.

Clear communication is essential to the success of a fund-raising campaign. People give to a need they understand, so it is important to show an artist's renderings of the proposed buildings, floor plans, and master site plan. Providing adequate information will encourage members to support the project, including with their pocketbooks.

Churches that conduct capital campaigns generally raise between one and three times their annual budget receipts. Churches that raise funds for construction projects collect more funds than those retiring debt or purchasing land. Churches that are raising money for educational space generally collect more than those that are building recreation or fellowship space. Churches that are raising funds for worship construction or relocation projects tend to collect the most.

The success of a capital campaign depends on the perceived need by the congregation. If members understand and share the urgency of the project, they will be much more likely to support it financially. For this reason any communication about the project needs to reinforce the why as well as the what.

BORROWING FOR THE PROJECT

The third option for funding a project is to borrow for it. This is typically one of the most volatile subjects surrounding a project. Some people have a biblical objection to borrowing, citing passages that discourage it and admonish believers to avoid debt. Others take a different approach, stating that the Bible refers to owing something and refusing to pay instead of an agreement between two parties to repay over time. We do not have space here to fully discuss these issues, so for now we will consider relevant issues for churches that decide to borrow.

If the church borrows, its total indebtedness should not exceed about 2 to 2½ times its regular budget receipts. A more precise rule of thumb is that the total payments for all loans should not exceed 20 to 25 percent of the church's annual income.

The object of both of these guidelines is to keep the church from overextending and having to reduce or eliminate ministries or even staff to pay its debt. Excessive debt can severely handicap the church and cause it not only to struggle to meet its financial obligations but also to lose focus on the ministries that required the project in the first place. If money becomes the focus, the church is in trouble.

A few years back, churches borrowed the money to build, either from a bank or by selling bonds. Bonds have lost favor as the preferred method of borrowing because of the problems of churches that wanted to pay off their bonds early. The bondholders were making a good fixed interest rate, and if the prevailing rate was lower, they were forced to reinvest at a lower rate. Of course, bond purchasers wanted a good rate of return on their money, and the church wanted the lowest possible interest rate. If the church members also happened to be the bondholders, a conflict of interest arose.

When capital fund-raising programs became popular in the 1960s, churches learned that selling bonds competed with the capital campaign for the same dollars. People who might have given $10,000 to the building instead bought a bond with that money. With interest the church ended up repaying the bonds over time at 150 to 200 percent of the amount borrowed instead of receiving a gift of that amount.

If your church decides to sell bonds, set two ground rules to avoid these issues: sell the bonds outside the church, and be sure there is no penalty for early repayment.

Excessive debt can severely handicap the church.

A Sample Project Budget

The typical fund-raising scenario looks something like this example. Community Church, with an annual undesignated income of $750,000, plans to build an educational addition. They conduct a capital campaign and receive covenant cards totaling $1.4 million (1.87 times their income). They decide to borrow $1.8 million (2.4 times their income). Since they also had $60,000 in the bank before the project started, this

SOFT COSTS

Additional items besides the building construction. These costs may include site preparation, paving for parking, furnishings, audiovisual systems, equipment, architectural and engineering design fees, materials testing during construction, extending utilities to the site, zoning and building-permit fees, impact fees, and a contingency amount for miscellaneous items.

BUILDING PERMIT

A certificate provided by a government giving permission to undertake a given construction project, usually issued after a comprehensive review of architectural drawings to ensure compliance with current codes and safety practices.

gives them a total of $3,260,000 for their project budget. Many churches would make the mistake of calling this figure the building budget and tell their architect to design a $3.2 million building. This decision could be a huge mistake because of soft costs.

In addition to the cost of construction, a church always need to account for additional items in the budget that usually amount to around 25 to 30 percent of the project budget. The total of funds calculated above is the total project budget. These are all of the funds available for the project. Soft costs are additional items besides the building construction. These budget items vary from project to project but generally include things like site preparation, paving for parking, furnishings, audiovisual systems, equipment, architectural and engineering design fees, materials testing during construction, extending utilities to the site, zoning and building-permit fees, impact fees, and a contingency amount for miscellaneous items. Soft costs tend to be highest in a relocation project and in areas where government entities are most stringent; soft costs are lower for additions to an existing building.

So if Community Church estimates these expenses to be about $880,200 (27 percent of the project budget), this leaves them with only about $2,379,800 to build a building. If that building costs about $130 per square foot, they can afford an 18,306-square-foot building. Had they not accounted for the soft costs, they might have designed a $4,000,000, 25,000-square-foot building they would not have been able to afford. They would have to pay the architect several thousand dollars to redesign it to fit it in the budget or go deep into debt to build it.

It is imperative that the project be designed to fit a budget that is calculated to include all expenses. Overextending the church into debt can have very harmful consequences. One church found itself with a load of debt so great that it had to dismiss several staff members. One strategic mistake caused a ripple effect that hampered this otherwise great church for the next 20 years. Ministry was difficult with little or no funds to do the work because almost all of the income had to go toward the debt.

Obtain a Good Master Plan

Once the needs have been identified, you still need a context for your building. Are there existing buildings to connect to? Will there be other buildings added in the future? What are the relationships to parking, street views, entrances and exits, and other site features? To answer these questions, every church needs a master plan for the development of its property. Whether this plan is the last phase of construction or the first on your property, you need to establish these contextual parameters and design the building to fit into the big picture of the property.

BENEFITS OF A MASTER PLAN

A plan of stewardship for your property. Be sure your church has a valid plan for the stewardship for all the land you own. This plan should include the location of all current and future educational, worship, recreational, parking, and other space.

A growth-driven strategy for your facilities. The plan unfolds at key milestones that are triggered by the growth of the church. As the church grows to fill up one phase, the plan shows you what to build next.

A financially feasible plan for the buildings the church will need in order to grow. Each phase is planned so that it fits the financial capacity of your church at that stage of growth. It is simple to project the revenue and the church's ability to fund a project at each juncture in the plan. When each phase is outgrown, the next should be feasible.

MASTER PLAN

A comprehensive plan for the physical growth of the church facilities to the saturation of the available property.

FUTURE MINISTRIES EXPANSION

An investment in the future of your church. Effective planning will make it possible to use the property efficiently. The return on investment for a master plan is in terms of preserving the growth potential of the church. Lost potential is poor stewardship. Future generations will thank you for considering their needs as well as your own.

A means of avoiding costly mistakes. If the church builds without considering where and when other building phases will be constructed, it could compromise the growth potential of the church. A good master plan will pay for itself in funds saved. By keeping the church from paving parking where a future building will go or making even more costly mistakes, the plan can save thousands of dollars.

A representation of your long-range vision. Once the congregation sees the master plan, it will begin to understand where the church is going. The facility is a physical representation that makes the church's vision more concrete and understandable.

ENGINEERING

A profession that uses technical, scientific, and mathematical knowledge to design certain aspects of a building project.

The best person to help you with a master plan is an experienced church architect with a Kingdom perspective.

Jesus said to whom much is given, much will be expected (see Luke 12:48). God entrusted property to your church with the expectation that it be used wisely and bear fruit. The only way to accomplish that is to be purposeful about using your property.

Many churches have a master plan that is no longer valid because they have not built according to the plan, they have purchased additional property, or the ministry has changed. Some churches have a plan provided by a planner who didn't fully understand the needs. If the plan didn't take into consideration things like balanced capacities for various age groups, such as preschool, beyond the first phase, you may need a new or updated plan. It should indicate at what milestones of growth you will need to build each phase of construction. It should take into consideration whether you will employ multiple worship services, locate recreational facilities, and provide a plan to maintain about two parking spaces per person in attendance throughout the plan.

If your church does not have a valid master plan, obtaining one should become a part of the planning process before building. This essential step could save you many thousands of dollars and create a significantly more effective ministry-oriented facility plan.

The best person to help you with a master plan is an experienced church architect with a Kingdom perspective. Not all architects can do good church master planning. You need someone who can quickly grasp the big picture of your ministry and how the existing buildings and other future buildings fit into that picture. It is so much more than placing buildings on a site. See appendix 7 (p. 222) for ways to contact LifeWay Architecture for help with a master plan. LifeWay has done more master planning for churches than any architectural firm in the country and knows how to get it right.

The master plan should include the programming for and conceptual design of the first phase of the plan. This will usually include only the site plan, floor plans, and perhaps an artist's rendering of the building to provide a concept of how the building will look. Detailed planning will come later, but you need some direction to rally around in the early stages of planning and to begin communicating the project to the congregation. You should not have to sign a contract for complete architectural service to get this.

The master plan should go beyond architecture or engineering, representing a comprehensive plan for the growth of the facilities to the saturation of the available property. More than just the locations of buildings, it should point out the types of spaces that will be needed and how these spaces will relate to one another and to existing facilities.

Avoid designing a collection of independent structures. Many churches are built so that each phase looks different from the others without unifying elements. All of the buildings don't have to match; but they should complement one another, each one a part of the whole.

The church's master plan should consider the way people enter the property, where they park, how they approach the building(s), and how they move from one part of the building(s) to another. A good master plan helps you avoid the mazelike hallways that are problems in some church buildings.

The plan should group classrooms by age groups and functions, avoiding a disorganized hodgepodge that can give people a feeling of discomfort and disorientation. Avoid creating obstacles to circulation through the building and funneling traffic through areas that should be secure, such as offices and preschool areas.

Plan the buildings with multiple services in mind for the best stewardship and consider the affordability of each construction phase so that each one is feasible in its time. Instead of letting current practice dictate the church's future, create flexible spaces so that they can get maximum use long-range.

Apply for Zoning

As soon as a building project has been defined, many churches need to apply for zoning approval. This should happen while the church raises money for the building. The application process can take many months in some jurisdictions, so start early and be patient. You may need legal assistance and/or the assistance of an architect and a civil engineer. For some churches, zoning is not an issue; but do not assume that to be the case. Contact your city or county government long before you are ready to begin building to learn whether zoning approval is needed.

The Capital-Stewardship Campaign

The next step is to start raising money for the project in earnest. There is no substitute for an organized campaign to systematically ensure that you have maximized the giving potential of the congregation. Employ an experienced consultant who can assist you in making this a spiritually driven, prayer-powered, Bible-centered experience in the life of the church, like the Beyond Measure® campaigns that LifeWay Stewardship offers. Your campaign will basically be a one-shot opportunity to raise the funds you need to do what God has called you to do, so it pays to get professional, experienced help.

There is no substitute for an organized campaign to maximize the giving potential of the congregation.

The old saying "It takes money to make money" might apply to a capital campaign. Investing a bit more in the presentation of the project to demonstrate that the committee has a commitment to the project, the project is worth investing in, and the project is important to the church will help you communicate to the congregation that this proposal is not just a sideline diversion but a key to ministry. The way you approach the giving program will communicate whether you as leaders believe it is important or optional. To approach the capital campaign apologetically or without a plan for clear communication to the church conveys the message that the project is elective or only for rich members to support. The message behind capital fund-raising should be that the project is both critical and the responsibility of all members. If the building is going to be an essential part of your church's vision, you need to state that not once but many times.

After the covenant cards have been turned in, it is the time to determine whether the project budget you outlined earlier in the process is going to be adequate. If the funds meet the estimate, the project can stay on course. If they come in below your earlier estimate, adjust the budget now before the project goes into the detailed design stages.

The Professional Team

SELECTING AN ARCHITECT

Architects' fees are fairly consistent, generally ranging between 5 and 8 percent of the cost of new construction. For the same project there will be little variation among architects. Assuming different architects will provide the same scope of services, the fees for various firms will usually vary by less than 1 percent of the project cost from the highest to the lowest. For this reason it is wise not to select the architect primarily on the basis of fees but on qualifications. If all of the architects are within a small range of fees, the right architect—one who can best interpret the church's needs and translate them into functional, attractive facilities—can be worth paying a little more to get on your team. A good architect might even allow you to gain even more than a 1 or 2 percent increase in the efficiency of the building, thus paying for the difference that way. An architect who charges a little less but delivers a much less efficient building that compromises your ministry is no bargain.

Good architects can save you from spending money in the wrong places and can help you get more from your construction dollars.

Most architects price their services according to the amount of time they will spend on the project, and they budget the hours they will spend according to the fee they charge. If the project takes longer than they budgeted, they lose money. An architect who charges the lowest fee may also plan to spend the fewest hours on the project to get it right, to make it beautiful, and to make his client happy. So the lowest fee may mean you get the worst service. If you save 1 percent on the architect but get 10 percent less building, the church has lost. Good architects can save you from spending money in the wrong places and can help you get more from your construction dollars.

Most churches should select an architect on the basis of experience; knowledge of the building type; design talent; passion for the project; and, of course, fee. Look at the architect's body of work. Talk to the churches they have worked with. Get to know the architect and understand his heart before deciding whether you want to form a partnership that will last two, three, or more years. As you get to know the architect, his relationship with the Lord will be evident, and that ought to have an impact on your decision. Someone who understands the mission of the church and is driven by the same desire to fulfill the Great Commission would be a great person to partner with you in a major project but only if he also meets the other qualifications.

Some architects have a reputation for ignoring their clients' budget and designing attractive buildings that the clients accept. Most churches are not in a position to be that flexible with their budgets. Before signing a contract with an architect, find out what his reputation is for meeting budgets.

Some architects will try to impose their will on your church, making it a monument to themselves, or will try to create what they think a church should look like. It may be an attractive sculptural edifice; but if it doesn't function as an effective tool to facilitate your ministry, it will frustrate your church's mission. On the other hand, some architects act as draftsmen, expecting you to do most of the design and just drawing what you describe. You are not getting your money's worth with either type. Great Commission churches need a true partner in ministry, an architect who can discern the functions they need to address, wrap it in a cost-effective but attractive envelope, and administer the construction process for quality control.

You should be able to rely on your architect to suggest designs that improve the function of the building. A good professional who understands architectural principles can work with your team to design a better building than you could, in terms of both function and beauty. The right architect can be the key to the success of the entire project.

The right architect can be the key to the success of the entire project.

OTHER DESIGNERS

Typically, the architect will bring engineers on board, who will design the many technical aspects of the building to make the design work, like plumbing lines, air-conditioning systems, the foundation and structural framework, and other details.

BID

An offer to provide goods or services for a given price, submitted for the purpose of comparison with other bids from other providers for the same goods or services.

CONSTRUCTION DOCUMENTS

Drawings, specifications, and supporting data that describe a project to be built.

A civil engineer will be required for most projects that involve any site design. You may wish to contract directly with this professional, who will design the drainage and paving, storm-water management, and other elements. Your architect will help you select an appropriate firm and may include these services in his fee. However, be aware that when one service is included under the contract of another professional, the fee will usually be marked up. Churches that need to save every penny can create separate contracts but will have more work to do in selecting and coordinating these services.

Other professionals might include interior designer, surveyor, legal counsel, real-estate broker, environmental engineer, geotechnical engineer, acoustical consultant, kitchen consultant, telephone/communications/computer-network consultant, landscape architect, security/alarm-system designer, sound-reinforcement and video consultant, and theatrical-lighting consultant. These roles are discussed in appendix 4 (p. 202). Work with your architect to determine which designers are needed for your project.

Design to Your Budget

When you select your architect, make it clear that the project should be designed to fit within the project budget. Explain the total project budget and the lower amount you have set as the construction budget. You will need to continue working with your architect to determine how much of the budget can be spent on the building and how much on soft costs. Be specific, because different architects will include different items in the soft costs. Some will not even include their own fees!

As the architect designs the building, he will give the leadership team several opportunities to review and influence the design. It is very important that church leaders be open and honest with the architect at each step, stating exactly what you like and do not like about the design. Everyone will not like everything. Compromises usually have to be made from time to time; but if you do not discuss the plan openly, you may find out too late that something could have been done to make the design better.

The best time to influence the design is at the preliminary floor-plan stage. Everything else will develop from this plan, so if you get it right, you increase your chances of having a great design. As each new drawing is presented, carefully examine it and make any changes needed at that time. Waiting until later to look more closely will probably add to the expense since the complexity grows and more things have to be changed to accommodate your alterations. At the floor-plan stage if you move a wall, you have moved only a wall. In the construction-documents stage if you move a wall, you may move not only the wall but also doors, windows, plumbing, the HVAC system, structural columns or beams, the foundation, electrical wiring and outlets, and more.

It rarely happens, but the goal should be to make changes only on the new information presented at each new stage of drawing development. Avoid going back and changing things that have already been approved. Some changes are appropriate and necessary. Others can be avoided if you pay careful attention at each step of the design.

Delivery Systems

As your construction project moves from the preliminary stages into the design stage, you will need to decide what delivery system you will use for the project. The three basic types of delivery systems are traditional design-bid-build; design-build; and integrated project delivery, or negotiated contracts.

TRADITIONAL DESIGN-BID-BUILD

In this delivery method the architect works with the church client to develop a design solution. The architect completes construction documents and then sends them out to multiple general contractors. Each contractor prices the construction and submits sealed bids for the church to examine and compare. The church has the option to accept or reject any or all of the bids.

DESIGN-BID-BUILD

A method of project delivery in which the architect completes construction documents and sends them out to multiple general contractors, who submit sealed bids for the job.

DESIGN-BUILD

A method of project delivery
in which architectural
services and construction
of the project are both
provided through a
single source provider.

Although design-bid-build has the apparent advantage of competitive bidding to get the best possible price, many churches have run into unexpected problems with this delivery system. The primary disadvantage is that the architect designs the project without the benefit of any substantive feedback on the cost. It would be similar to shopping without knowing the prices of any goods you are buying. When you go to the checkout, you may be surprised by the total cost of what you've picked out.

At this point, just when the congregation is anticipating the groundbreaking for the building, the church might have to negotiate with one of the contractors to make last-minute changes that keep the project within the budget. Sometimes it requires major changes in the building design, which can require literally going back to the drawing board and can incur significant charges from the architect and/or engineers.

Churches have successfully used this method for years, but it requires great self-control and discipline throughout the design process. The best way to avoid catastrophe is to include items in the design that can be eliminated at the last minute without compromising the function of the project. It takes forethought and skill to achieve the right amount of flexibility, especially since you do not know the prices of the contingency items; but in the design-bid-build system this method is the safest way to ensure that the project will not have to be shelved after bids are in.

DESIGN-BUILD

Recently, many churches have used a method of project delivery commonly called design-build. Some firms refer to it as construction management at risk, but these are practically the same to the church. This approach frequently involves getting a guaranteed maximum price (GMP) for the project very early in the schematic or design-development phase. In this delivery system the church employs one firm that handles both the design and the construction of the building in order to reduce costs and to stick to a project budget that is established early in the process.

RISKS OF DESIGN-BUILD

The church doesn't get to choose the architect for the project. The design-build firm makes that call, so an inexperienced architect might be hired to design your building.

The plans the architect draws for a design-build are usually less comprehensive than conventional plans. Some details are intentionally omitted from the drawings to be worked out on the job. Specifications may be very broad and open to the interpretation of the supplier or subcontractor in order to get lower prices.

Because the contractor has guaranteed the final construction price before the project documents are completed, he must find a way to keep costs within that price. Since the contractor gets to keep any amount left over, not only is the pressure on to deliver the building on budget, but there is also a temptation to reduce the quality of the project in order to increase profits.

Once the contractor begins to build your building, it is the architect's role to periodically inspect the construction to make sure it is being accomplished as indicated on the drawings and specifications. There are two problems here: (1) If the documents are less specific, there is less control over how the building gets built. (2) The architect is either the owner of or employed by the design-build firm. Any work he requires to be corrected will cost his firm or his employer's firm to fix. The conflict of interest is clear: the architect is torn between his duty to give you a quality building and his motive of producing higher profits for himself or his employer. It takes great integrity to tell your boss that he has to tear out a wall and replace the insulation or make other corrections, especially when the church would probably never find out!

The bottom line is that, although the cost may be less with design-build, there is considerable risk that the quality of the building can be compromised in design quality and execution as compared to other arrangements, unless the design-builder is extremely trustworthy or the church is extremely knowledgeable about the details of commercial

GENERAL CONTRACTOR

A company or individual in overall control of the construction process. There may be several subcontractors whom the contractor employs to work under this agreement to accomplish the work, but the general contractor is usually the only party to contract with the church for construction.

SPECIFICATIONS

A textural description defining the quality and standards for the major elements and workmanship that go into a building project.

SUBCONTRACTOR

A person or entity working for a general contractor to provide construction services of a certain part of a project, such as concrete or steel.

construction. Even then the church should very carefully weigh the wisdom of putting the church's well-being in the hands of anyone who has so much to gain from making compromises to the construction methods and materials used in your building. Advocates of design-build claim that it's the best way to save money on a project. That's true if you totally trust the contractor to design and build a quality building and to decide which cuts are made to achieve those savings.

NEGOTIATED CONTRACTS, OR INTEGRATED PROJECT DELIVERY

In the negotiated contract form of project delivery, the relationships among the church, the architect, and the contractor are about the same as in the traditional design-bid-build system but with one key difference. Rather than waiting to bid out the project after the architect has finished the construction documents, the contractor is employed through an interview process early in the design stage. Your architect will usually participate in the interviews and assist in the selection process.

The success rate of negotiated contracts has been so high over the past 20 years that its popularity has increased. This method has several advantages for most church projects.

THE CONTRACTOR IS INVOLVED in the process much earlier and can use his cost-estimating skills to assist the architect and the church as the design is being completed.

AT EACH STAGE OF DESIGN, THE PROJECT IS PRICED by a qualified person who is prepared to deliver on that price.

THERE IS A GREAT DEAL OF COMPETITION AT THE SUBCONTRACTOR LEVEL. The general contractor you choose will submit the plans to multiple subcontractors, who bid against one another at the conclusion of the construction-documents phase.

THE ACCOUNTABILITY BETWEEN THE ARCHITECT AND THE CONTRACTOR remains in place, so there is not the "fox watching the henhouse" fear that goes with design-build.

THE CHURCH CAN GET THE SAME KIND OF SAVINGS as they would in a design-build, but the church and architect have the ability to control where the savings are achieved.

Integrated project delivery (IPD) is a variation on this arrangement, and there are many variations within this system. In some IPD and negotiated-contract arrangements, the owner, the architect, and/or the contractor share in any savings below the estimated cost of construction. This calls for a "cost-plus, with a guaranteed maximum price" contract that divides the savings among the parties. This means the church pays the actual cost of construction up to a certain figure. If the actual cost is less than that amount, the difference is divided among the parties responsible for the savings. For the most effective cost control, the contractor should be involved early in the process. For the most effective quality control, the contractor and architect should be kept as separate interests, each contracted independently and accountable to the church.

Even if well designed with early estimates of costs, your project can still exceed your budget. Many variables in the products and methods of construction are not determined until the completion of the final construction drawings. Prices can be very volatile. Sometimes subcontractors will not guarantee prices for more than a week, so prices obtained at the early stages of the design can change by the time the drawings are finished. Then what?

> ### NEGOTIATED CONTRACT
>
> A project-delivery method in which the contractor and the architect are both hired directly and independently by the project owner during the design process and the contract amount for construction is adjusted and negotiated as the design process continues. Generally used as a method of ensuring that a project stays within budget when the owner desires a high level of control over the quality of the construction.

VALUE ENGINEERING

The process of making and evaluating recommendations for increasing the economic efficiency of a project.

Value Engineering

After several reviews and development of the plans, the architect will complete the drawings (sometimes called blueprints) and specifications for the project and will be ready to issue them for final pricing and permitting. As the drawings and specifications are completed, the contractor should provide feedback about the cost of the project. As the contractor reviews the documents, he should suggest ways to save money on the building, normally by providing a list of items that can be changed or deleted from the project and an amount that can be saved by accepting that item. This feedback process, referred to as value engineering (sometimes called VE), can begin as early as a floor plan is designed and continues through the completion of the drawings.

An experienced contractor will have many ideas. Some will be great ideas you can take immediately, while others may require research to evaluate. Your architect should review each item because he may know a good reason to accept or reject an item that your committee does not know about. Some ideas will be rejected as unsuitable, and others will be accepted only if the project is seriously over budget and there are no other alternatives to achieve your budget limit. Once the drawings and specifications are complete, a final round of feedback and value engineering may be needed.

Even in a negotiated contract, when the architect completes the construction documents and the final pricing is received, the church will need to evaluate and determine whether it will continue to work with the preselected contractor to carry out the construction. In the event you do not, you will have the option to bid out the project at that time. For this reason the agreement with the original contractor should include a buyout clause in the case the church is not satisfied with the performance of the contractor during the design stage. This buyout should be a very modest amount. Most contractors have a zero-fee buyout because they feel they should be able to earn your confidence as you work with them during the value-engineering process, and if you are not satisfied, you should not feel obligated to stay with them.

Bidding and Negotiation

If your church did not select a contractor early in the process, you will need to place the project out for bids at this time. Your architect can help you invite bidders and distribute the documents and an invitation to bid. After an appropriate time (usually two to four weeks) for the contractors to contact their subcontractors and assemble their bids, the bids should be sealed and delivered so that all can be opened at the same time. The bids are opened at a meeting at which the contractors can see and hear their competitors' bids. The church then selects which company to contract with. You should not automatically take the lowest bidder but investigate the subcontractors to be used and the general contractor's track record before negotiating and contracting with one.

The negotiations may include some last-minute value engineering, particularly if it has not been done up to this point. The contractor you have selected will want you to sign a contract for constructing the building. This binding agreement will state exactly what the contractor will do. A one- or two-page agreement is not adequate for this task. The architect's plans and specifications should be specifically referred to in the contract for construction and should become part of the contract.

The safest way to get a fair, thorough agreement that will protect you and the contractor in a relationship is to use standard contract documents like those published by the American Institute of Architects (AIA). These contracts have been tested in the courts, have been used for many years, and have been improved over time. Contractor-written contracts and those of other origins have not been used as extensively and therefore are not proven. They could be biased, vague, or even legally nonbinding in court if the worst should happen. Have a lawyer review all contracts related to your building project. No one wants to go to court or even mediation for that matter; but if you do, you will want to have a tested, fair, and neutral instrument outlining the agreement and describing the role each party is supposed to fulfill. Without it you are at the mercy of others who may not be sympathetic toward the church.

The safest way to get a fair, thorough agreement is to use standard contracts like those published by the American Institute of Architects.

Bonding

The church will have the option to require the contractor to obtain a bond. The cost is much less than the potential loss, but the risk of needing to file a claim is hard to determine. Your relationship with the contractor, his track record, and the church's risk tolerance in general will determine whether a bond is required. There are three types of bonds for the church to consider.

A BID BOND is purchased by the low bidder to ensure that the church will be paid the difference between the low bid and the next lowest bid if the low bidder should fail to undertake the project.

A PERFORMANCE BOND is a guarantee that the contractor will complete the building project as designed. Usually, the contractor, who has an ongoing relationship with the bonding company, pays for the bond but passes the expense on to the church. If the contractor becomes insolvent, goes out of business, declares bankruptcy, or for any other reason does not complete the project, the bonding company pays the church the amount needed to complete the project up to the amount of the bond.

A PAYMENT BOND is usually issued with the performance bond to ensure that the contractor will pay all suppliers and subcontractors. If the contractor fails to pay any of these, the bond company pays them. The primary reason churches want a payment bond is to eliminate a contractor's potential to file a lien against the church's property, which is what typically happens if the contractor or subcontractor does not get paid.

Some churches use alternative strategies to avoid paying for bonds. One approach is to get the contractor to price the bond. If the contractor has a good track record, the cost of the bond will not be very high. Some will not be able to get a bond for the size project you are building. With this information you know whether the contractor can qualify for the bond, and the church can then choose whether to pay for the bond. Even if you do not require it, you know the contractor qualified for it. That gives you some assurance that the company is stable since it qualified for the bond.

Instead of a payment bond, churches sometimes require releases of lien from the major subcontractors prior to payment each month. These releases are notarized legal statements submitted by the subcontractors that they have been paid and will not file a lien on the church's property. This requirement needs to be written into the construction contract so that subcontractors know they will be required to submit the releases of lien monthly with their pay requests.

It is never wise to just trust that the contractor will take care of business and will not have to declare bankruptcy in the middle of your project. Requiring the performance and payment bond is the safest course of action.

Before addressing the construction phase, let's summarize key points discussed so far.

Develop a stewardship mind-set.

Create a good, ministry-driven master plan.

Maintain balance among age groups and among worship, education, and parking.

Adopt a realistic budget.

Stick to your budget by involving value engineering throughout the project.

RELEASE OF LIEN

A legal document, usually notarized, stating that a potential claimant will not file a lien on a property, usually indicating that all appropriate payment has been received.

CHAPTER 6

Construction

A new building's worth will be measured by
its eternal impact on the lives of people.

After the contractor has submitted costs and a period of negotiation and last-minute value engineering is complete, the contractor will submit the project to the authorities for permitting. Because building codes are subject to interpretation, the plans reviewer usually requests a few changes before issuing a building permit. The permitting process can take a day or many months, depending on the amount of construction and the level of scrutiny given by the building officials. Some check plans at many levels, including zoning, a building official, a fire marshal, landscaping, and urban forestry. Each of these may require changes to the design before granting the permit.

Once the permit is granted, it's time for a celebration!

Groundbreaking

Groundbreaking for the new structure is a milestone event in the life of the church, not because it marks the accomplishment of ministry but because it represents the culmination of a great deal of effort toward a goal by many people.

The groundbreaking celebration should be just that—a party! A milestone reached is a time to give thanks to God for bringing the church to this significant moment. It can be included in a regular worship service, but most churches plan a separate ceremonial groundbreaking, with the congregation present to witness the turning of soil.

Because the groundbreaking ceremony is usually held outside, it should be kept fairly brief. It should include a lot of prayer, with different people assigned to mention different topics in their prayers. Here are some suggestions.

GIVE THANKS for the people God has used to bring the project to this point, including the planning and fund-raising teams.

GIVE THANKS for those who have given to the project, no matter the size of the gift.

GIVE THANKS for your architect, engineers, contractor, and others whom God has brought into the life of your church to help you plan and prepare for this moment.

PRAY FOR WISDOM as the team continues to make many decisions that will arise during the construction process.

PRAY FOR THE SAFETY of construction workers and for a positive impact on them.

PRAY FOR GOD TO GRANT FAVOR during the construction process through favorable weather and to allow the work to pass inspections and receive a certificate of occupancy without delay.

PRAY FOR FUTURE MINISTRY that will take place and lives that will be touched in and through the new church facility.

Intersperse songs of celebration and thanksgiving, introduce key people the congregation may not know, and deliver a brief word about the vision God has given for using the facility to impact the church and community.

The climax of the celebration should be the actual turning of a shovel of soil. Some churches use a shovel painted gold, but the main point is to symbolically represent the reality that this building project involves the entire congregation. For this reason representatives of each age group, each ministry area, and various lengths of church membership should participate in the groundbreaking ceremony. You can use several shovels or have participants pass one shovel along as each turns the soil.

A milestone reached is a time to give thanks to God for bringing the church to this significant moment.

SUPERINTENDENT

A contractor's representative at a project site who gives day-to-day guidance to the overall construction process.

Construction Progress

At this point the process is far from over, but if you have done your job well, the project has reached a level of momentum that will take much less energy to keep going. With the right contractor and architect on your team, the project will stay on a schedule and will maintain its own forward motion.

The construction phase may begin with a preconstruction meeting. The contractor, main subcontractors, the architect, and the owner's representative meet and go over the construction schedule and review any outstanding issues that need to be addressed.

The contractor should employ a superintendent to be on-site to guide the work and run the project whenever work is in progress. An assistant may be designated to take over when the superintendent cannot be there. The contractor should provide you with a schedule of values to show the amount to be paid for each part of the work.

It is also important that the church clearly designate one person to be the official spokesperson to communicate with the architect and the contractor. If this contact is not clear or is circumvented, it will cause confusion and could allow costly mistakes to creep into the project. The architect and the contractor should not accept answers from anyone else. Consistency in this area is very important.

The contractor will give you samples and drawings of the components for approval. These submittals and shop drawings should be reviewed by the architect.

It is important that questions and answers go through the architect. If some questions come through the architect and some do not, there is the potential for disaster. The architect should be the clearinghouse for all project information. The contractor or the church does not always know the reasons behind decisions and selections that have been made, and bypassing the architect can mean making a decision based on incomplete, conflicting, or wrong information. Keeping the architect in the loop is the best way to avoid adding errors to the project.

No construction project is perfect. No set of construction documents is perfect. Issues will arise during construction that will need to be resolved. Be patient and be prepared to deal with them. Some will cost money. For this reason we recommend keeping at least a 2 to 5 percent contingency fund in reserve during the construction of the building. As the project is completed, you will be glad you have budgeted a little money to resolve these issues. One of the most common cost overruns is for excavation. If the project runs into unexpected rock that has to be blasted out of the ground, its removal is usually not built into the project, and the church will pay extra for it.

Change orders are one of the most dreaded fears about a project. These documents authorize a change in the cost of the project budget. Some are for items that are necessary to the project but were not called for or understood from the drawings. Some are generated when the church requests changes at the last minute.

Change-order items are perceived to be more expensive than the same items would have been if included in the original contract amount, but this is usually not the case. It may appear that way because the requests are seen in isolation.

Regardless of the source, when you are not expecting a cost increase, a last-minute increase of any amount is not considered good news. The best way to avoid negative surprises is to have a good set of construction documents by your architect and a detail-oriented contractor who follows the drawings. Sometimes a bid that is low on a project is low because items were left out that will need to be added to get the real apples-to-apples price for the building. As you compare bids, look for large discrepancies that may indicate omissions. Even if they are unintentional, they can cost you in the form of a change order. Keeping a contingency budget is a good hedge against these costs. For more information about change orders, see appendix 5, page 216.

The architect should be the clearinghouse for all project information.

Pay Requests

REQUEST FOR PAYMENT
(pay request)

A document submitted by
a contractor certifying that
certain tasks have been
completed and materials
have been purchased
and stored securely and
requesting that the owner
pay the contracted amount.

Usually once a month the architect will receive a pay request from the contractor. This request is a document that authenticates that the contractor has completed certain portions of the work and is due payment on that portion, less a certain retainage (usually 5 to 10 percent). The architect will review the pay request either by personally visiting the site, viewing receipts, or receiving photographic or other evidence that the work is done and/or materials have been delivered and securely stored on the site. Then the architect will forward the pay request to the church for payment.

The retainage is held by the church and is not paid until the end of the project to ensure that the contractor completes the project.

Pay requests should always be paid as quickly as possible to facilitate the cash flow for the project. If the cash flow is not prompt, it can demotivate subcontractors and can tempt them to work on another project that pays more promptly.

Furnishings

Early in the project the church should begin planning furnishings for the building. This can take time for selection, ordering, production, and delivery, so it is important to gauge the time required to have the furnishings when they are needed. If they are delivered too soon, you may have to store them for a long time. Items like pews, sound systems, and lighting cannot wait until the last second, so work with your provider and the contractor to time their delivery when they are needed.

Enlarge the Organization

Another item that needs to be addressed as the building is being constructed is leadership for new classes. When churches construct new buildings, most plan to grow their organizational models as well as the numbers of people. That will mean more teachers need to be trained and outreach leaders need to be recruited. This process is all part of the enlargement of the church and a key to promoting numerical growth.

Hopefully, while the building is being planned and constructed, you have communicated the message that the building will not grow the church but is just a tool for ministry. The ministry of Jesus Christ through the church will make a difference in people's lives. Now comes the time to implement that ministry.

A new building without an enlarged organization with trained, skilled workers will not reach its potential to impact the church and community. Begin now to enlist, train, and prepare leaders for the day when a new building will allow them to play a key role in changing lives through expanded and enhanced ministries.

Construction Issues

As the construction progresses, many small decisions will need to be made. The team in charge of the project needs to remain available to respond quickly to these issues and to keep the project moving forward.

Once the building begins to take shape, it will be tempting to start moving in and using the slab, the building, or portions of it for various functions. A construction site, however, can be a very dangerous place. If possible, the site should be fenced off or locked, and the general public should stay out of the construction area until a building official inspects and approves the project. Be aware that potential problems like the following can result from early occupancy of an incomplete or uninspected building.

RETAINAGE

A portion of the payment due to the contractor, usually 5 to 10 percent, held by the church until after construction is completed.

SUBSTANTIAL COMPLETION

The point in a building project when approximately 90 percent of the work is complete and the owner can take occupancy.

THE CHURCH WOULD ASSUME CONSIDERABLE RISK by occupying or using the building before substantial completion because some safety issues may not have been identified. If the building is far enough along and such risks are not present, the authorities might be willing to issue a temporary certificate of occupancy. If this permission is not possible, the church would not be wise to take on this unnecessary risk. Regardless, if you choose to do something in an incomplete building, check with your insurance carrier to verify that you would be covered in case of personal injury or other damage.

IN THE EVENT SOME INADVERTENT OR MALICIOUS DAMAGE is done to the building while in a temporary or unauthorized occupancy, there could be problems determining who is responsible to correct the work. The contractor could claim that items were damaged during a church service when they were actually damaged by his own workers. If the church has used the facility, it would be very difficult to prove the contractor wrong and hold him accountable to make repairs.

Throughout the construction you will have the opportunity to inspect the progress with your architect to point out and discuss items that have not been completed to your satisfaction. These should all be reported to the architect, who will verify that it was called for in the documents and will relay the request to the contractor.

Usually, when the contractor says the building is about 90 percent complete, the project is deemed to be substantially complete. Then the architect will issue a certificate of substantial completion, which identifies the date the project has reached a point that the owner can use it. To achieve this milestone, the facility must be safe to use, and all of the key systems must be operational. A temporary certificate of occupancy will usually have to be obtained from the building official. The date of substantial completion establishes that warranties are activated. Typically, all work and materials will be guaranteed for one year from the time you take possession. The roof, equipment, windows, hardware, and other individual components will have additional warranties, but the clock begins ticking on all of them at substantial completion.

The Punch List

At this point the contractor, the church, and the architect work together to compile a list of things still to be completed and/or corrected. Once it is complete, the list is submitted to the contractor for his approval. This becomes his official to-do list for finishing the project, so make sure it is complete.

Leaving something off the punch list does not mean it doesn't have to be done, but it is wise to include a lot of detail on the list. The original construction documents are still the governing basis for the work, but this is an opportunity to assist the contractor and let him know what things you are looking for to call the job complete and to expedite the completion of items that may have been missed otherwise. The church should work with the architect to determine an appropriate amount of retainage to withhold for completing the work and for keeping the contractor motivated.

Once the punch list is complete and the church gets a temporary certificate of occupancy, the church can begin moving in. The punch list serves as a document to note the

---

PUNCH LIST

A list of all items remaining to be completed on a project, usually compiled at the substantial completion (90 percent) stage of construction.

exact condition of the building before you begin to occupy and use it. You can hold the contractor accountable for anything reported on the punch list prior to occupancy but not for any damage done after you occupy the building.

As soon as you take possession of the facility, the utilities will be transferred to the church, and your insurance will need to be in force. Be sure the contractor gives you the owner's manuals for all of the equipment and warranty papers for the products in the building because the church will need to operate and maintain them. Arrange for a walk-through with your contractor and/or architect to cite any warranty items that need attention a month before the one-year anniversary of taking possession.

Final Completion and Ownership

Finally, the contractor will apply and obtain the final certificate of occupancy. Once all items on the punch list have been addressed and a certificate of occupancy is obtained, the building project is complete. The point of final completion marks the time to pay all remaining balances due to the contractor.

This final phase, ownership, lasts much longer than any of the others. For the rest of the life of the building, you will pay the utilities and maintain the building. This is when you will be thankful if you have done a good job of building a sustainable structure that requires minimal maintenance and keeps utility bills low.

The true payoff for a job well done comes when the church implements the plans it has made to put the new facility to work by worshiping, by starting new units of Bible study, and by launching new ministries to impact lives for Christ. When dreams become reality and plans translate into changed lives and lost souls coming to Jesus, it makes all of the hours of planning and hard work worthwhile.

CERTIFICATE OF OCCUPANCY

A certificate issued by the government authority having jurisdiction that allows a public building such as a church to be used for the general population.

The Dedication Service

A dedication service is an appropriate way to celebrate the completion of the building project, to publicly announce to the community that the new building is open, and to publicly commit to God to use the facility for effective Kingdom ministry as He directs. Sometimes it is a good idea to delay the formal opening of the building even to church use until you have time for a few dress rehearsals. Especially in a new worship facility with new and unfamiliar technology and equipment, it would be a good idea for only the staff and the sound, lights, and video crews to rehearse several times before attempting a service with a live audience.

The next step might be to have a soft opening by holding a few regular services. The grand opening and dedication service should usually be held a few weeks afterward to ensure that everything works before the public opening. You can use this time to plan the event and to invite the media and dignitaries to be present. The grand opening gives you an opportunity to raise the church's visibility in the community.

The dedication service, an important component of the grand opening, should honor God as the source for all that has been accomplished and will be accomplished in the future. This service might also include a recognition of the planning team, a recognition of dignitaries, a prayer of dedication, a ribbon cutting, and tours of the building.

Once the building is in use, the work really begins! The ministry that your church planned can begin to have an impact, and the church can work toward its goals of reaching and ministering to people in new ways. A tool like a new building will be effective only if it is applied to the work for which it was intended.

As God guided you through this process, may He also bless you for your dedication and hard work in bringing your project about. May He impact lives through your church and through this new facility as never before!

Changed lives and lost souls coming to Jesus make all of the hours of planning and hard work worthwhile.

APPENDIXES

Screwtape on Church Building

WITH APOLOGIES TO C. S. LEWIS

In 1942 C. S. Lewis published a book of letters from a fictional senior demon named Screwtape to his nephew and junior demonic disciple, Wormwood, on how to do the bidding of their evil master by attacking his prey in sometimes subtle and insidious ways. The book serves to remind us that although demons are limited in power, they are clever and oh so wily. Here is an attempt to suggest some of the things a modern-day Screwtape would say to his charge about a church that enters a building campaign.

My horrible protégé,

It has come to my attention that your assigned human patient has been appointed as the leader of the church building committee. I understand that you were quite alarmed at this news, but I do not see this in itself as a failure on your part. Although it can be a setback for our cause, it can also be an opportunity. Many times the Evil One has used such a position of authority as a platform to accomplish his purpose. Now that your client is a leader, his increased visibility can be beneficial to us, particularly if you can properly distract him from his goals.

Remember first and foremost that our purpose for those who have already been saved from eternal damnation is to minimize the damage and keep them from spreading their detestable faith to others. We want to render them ineffective; complacent; or better yet, content to go happily on to heaven without the least concern for the condition of others' souls. Nothing inherent in a building guarantees that faith will spread. Properly addressed, a building project can be twisted into a sordid victory for our cause!

It is true that the mere existence of a building committee may be construed as a sign of a certain amount of success on the part of our enemy. Numerical growth is a common justification for this action, but it is not the only reason churches build. A building project, with its expenditures of great sums of money, can be turned against unsuspecting humans to stop and perhaps even reverse a disturbing growth trend. The subject of money almost always presents an opportunity for all kinds of ill effects we can bring to bear against the ones we hate. Greed is a powerful tool, and used correctly, it can demoralize even the best of saints.

The particular position your patient has been appointed to can make him particularly vulnerable to our attacks. As the leader of a building committee, he will be in unfamiliar territory, giving us the advantage. I have quite a bit of experience with these groups and have found them to be some of our better vehicles for disruption.

Building committees can be useful to us in several ways. For some reason mortals tend to think they cannot fail as long as they are working for the church. To actively pursue a project for the benefit of the church is enough to satisfy their spiritual appetite, so they can be led to neglect the disciplines of prayer and spiritual nourishment, in turn providing an opening for your attack. Keep them busy and focused on the details of the project, and time allocated to these spiritual endeavors may be reduced. Communication with the enemy will be cut off, and the humans will be left to their own devices to lead without God's wisdom and perspective to guide them.

You may be able to get a few outspoken carnal, backslidden members to misdirect the project if they are vocal enough. They do not have to be many, just enough to make significant noise in meetings so as to appear to be a powerful force. Most congregations find conflict distasteful, so they can be persuaded to give in to a few insistent voices. Add to this our proven tactic of keeping the committed ones silent, and you can take the congregation on a very expensive wild-goose chase! How delightful to see a congregation spend months and millions chasing false assumptions and selfish motives!

Postmodern congregations are very tolerant of all kinds of evil behavior from their fellow members—selfishness most of all. All you have to do is suggest that this is their opportunity to get what they want. If they are going to promote their agenda, it is now or never! Try to convince them that they deserve something in return for the money they have given—and no, it doesn't matter how much or how little they have given.

Jealousy is another delightful tool you can use to influence the process and to steer the project away from real needs. One method that has worked well is to have the building committee take tours of other facilities. Before long they see something they want, and that's the time to stoke the fires of envy and jealousy! If you can get them to desire what others have, you have them! They begin to promote their own agenda instead of what the church really needs.

It is most effective, however, if you can get them to couch their selfish, self-serving requests in spiritual terms. They can say the motive is to reach others or provide for their children or teenagers; but as long as it is not what the church really needs, it will accomplish our purpose. One thing that makes this strategy effective is that something that works well for one church might not work at all for another. Because of the differences in their programs, existing facilities, and call to ministry, building what another church did will almost always be a marvelous disaster.

An outward-focused congregation is a very dangerous thing. On the other hand, keeping members focused on themselves and getting them to cater only to their own progeny usually distract them from any real growth efforts. When we do our job right, not only will the church be distracted from its mission and spend thousands of dollars on facilities it doesn't need, but members will also teach their children that the church is there to serve them. When enjoyment and self-glorification become most important, churches overlook servanthood and outreach, focusing instead on providing pleasure instead of that wretched discipleship! Thus, they are prepared for a wonderful lifetime of selfishness and a misconception of the purpose of church!

Try to see to it that the church building committee meets often enough that the members cannot do the work of the church such as teaching, missions, and evangelism. All of these things we hate are reduced when leaders are distracted by the building process. The work of the church moves to the back burner while they focus on the building.

Even in the hands of a novice demon like yourself, this process of busyness and frustration without productivity can be stretched out for months and sometimes even years. As our great evil leader says, "The absence of fruit is our greatest delight!"

One way to prolong the process is to get leaders to make rash statements about unity and harmony. I have heard pastors say, "We will not do anything unless we all agree on it!" or "Members must approve this proposal by a 90 percent margin." When unrealistic expectations become the criteria, the church is much slower to act if it does anything at all. On the other hand, if it is truly unified, you will be in for a very tough time.

As a matter of fact, diverse ideas are one of our best tools to confuse and delay otherwise devoted followers. Throughout the process suggest a wide variety of solutions—the more, the better. One or more can even be correct; but if there are a number of different ideas, members won't be united and won't be able to move forward. At every turn give them options. Most congregations have a lot of different ideas, but the most dangerous congregations know how to narrow them down to a few good ones and eventually one best solution. Whatever you do, don't let them bring in outside help to sort out possibilities and narrow them down to the best solution. Try to avoid any outside help; but if you slip up and let this happen, try to involve someone with an agenda of his own rather than one focused on ministry.

Many companies claim to specialize in church solutions but actually victimize the church, seeing its leaders as easy prey and ignorant, poor decision makers who can be taken advantage of. These companies speak in spiritual terms and frequently offer discount prices. They might offer turnkey buildings to take decision making away from the leaders and to provide generic buildings that rarely fit the situation or maximize the church's resources. Steer the church toward one of these companies, whose true motive is to put money in their own pockets.

Also try to steer the church toward someone who is well meaning but inexperienced or incompetent, someone who wants to help the church but lacks the training or the means to do it. Such a person wastes the church's time and may even get it to build something it later regrets. It is so delightful to see a congregation spend hundreds of thousands of dollars on something it later regrets! Unlicensed do-it-yourselfers, design-build contractors, architects, general contractors, and consultants can be found that fit this description. Because they claim to care about the church and know what to do to help them, they are almost indistinguishable from those who really do.

Once a church is committed to working with one of these incompetent professionals, it has great difficulty admitting it made a bad decision and getting out of the relationship. Avoid letting the church sign on for a limited scope of service, because it might figure out its consultant's lack of knowledge and bail out. Get the church to commit fully and early, and you'll have a good chance to see one of the greatest rewards in our business: a complete set of blueprints for a building the church will never build or a church that builds the wrong building in the wrong place on its property, greatly limiting its future growth and wasting thousands (if not millions) of dollars.

When the church starts raising money for the construction project, be sure the campaign centers on the almighty dollar! Get the members to focus on themselves and what they can do, never on what God can do and has done. Right now, before the church starts asking for money, tempt members with material possessions that have a big price tag. If they are obligated to purchase or at least lust after possessions, they won't feel that they can give to the project. On the other hand, if you let the church start talking about stewardship and God's ownership, it can dissolve into a nauseatingly spiritual time of growth for the entire congregation.

Another great tactic is to segment the church by treating the rich in the church differently from the middle class and the poor, as if the latter have little or nothing to offer. Let the rich wield power but give little and let the others feel as if they are not needed or wanted, and you have a perfect recipe for failure!

However, I have seen these campaigns do more damage to our cause than a year of sermons, because they give the believers a chance to exercise their faith, not just talk about it. You must not let this happen. Use their greed, jealousy, and every tool you can think of to minimize the impact of a giving campaign.

Many humans we attack are prone to skepticism, which you can use to create doubt and restraint in their approach to giving. Feed their skepticism with rumors and poor communication, and you will make a dent in the funds that fuel the entire project. Good communication is detrimental to our cause, so keep the project vague and uninspiring. Sabotage communication, and the battle is half won!

One final piece of advice: use the moral failures of your newly appointed leader against him. Start now building an inventory of failures and sins to remind him of. If possible, tempt him in his most vulnerable spot at midcampaign; a moral failure in the middle of a project can be a huge victory for you. Not only will you earn our Evil Master's recognition for the moral downfall of a church leader, but you will also get credit for totally disrupting a critical project for the church! If a moral failure becomes known, your human will lose all credibility with his peers, and they will distrust all he has done, including his work on the project. Even if it does not become known, he will feel vulnerable and ashamed, hardly in a strong position to lead.

Do not go overboard with your temptations. As I told you before, our goal is not to send him spinning off to hell all at once but gradually, taking as many with him as possible. If your work becomes too heavy-handed and obvious, it can bring about repentance and a growing dependence on God, and we certainly don't want that!

In conclusion, my horrible protégé, see this as an opportunity to distract your assigned mortal and render him ineffective. Although he is being watched over by our enemy, if he gives you an opening, be ready to take it! Avoid the temptation to assume the battle is lost. No, it is far from over! Our old mortal enemy Winston Churchill once said, "We shape our buildings; and thereafter, they shape us."[1] If you can influence the shape of the church building, you can frustrate the future ministry of that congregation. What an opportunity!

Now go do your worst.

Your affectionate uncle,

Screwtape

1. Linda Wolcott, "As the Library Shapes Students, Students Shape the Library," *Marginalia* [online], 2006 [cited 10 February 2010]. Available from the Internet: *http://library.usu.edu.*

Glossary

ACOUSTICS: The study of sound and the built environment, including how sound travels through materials from one space into the next, as well as how sound behaves and is perceived within a particular space.

ALTAR: In the Old Testament an altar was a place to offer sacrifices. Today some people refer to the platform of the church as an altar.

ARCHITECTURE: A discipline that combines the art and science of designing a built environment. By classical definition, architecture integrates the three major components of beauty, function, and structural integrity.

BID: An offer to provide goods or services for a given price, submitted for the purpose of comparison with other bids from other providers for the same services or goods.

BUILDING PERMIT: A certificate provided by a government giving permission to undertake a given construction project, usually issued after a comprehensive review of architectural drawings to ensure compliance with current codes and safety practices.

BLUEPRINTS: A common term for the architectural plans for a project. Actually, blueprints are the result of a type of copy process that results in white lines on a blue background, but this method is no longer used in most areas. Today plans are reproduced using xerographic or electrostatic processes, resulting in black lines on white paper.

CAPITAL FUND-RAISING: The process of soliciting gifts for a specific project consisting of improvements to a physical plant. Most campaigns are modeled after the Together We Build® campaigns introduced in the 1960s. LifeWay Christian Resources still provides this campaign and many other types of fund-raising campaigns for churches.

CERTIFICATE OF OCCUPANCY: A certificate issued by the government authority having jurisdiction that allows a public building such as a church to be used for the general population.

CHANCEL: The platform area of a gothic-style church building or cathedral where worship leaders stand.

COLUMN: A vertical structural member that supports a beam or another structural member.

Construction Documents: Drawings, specifications, and supporting data that describe a project to be built.

Cornice: A decorative horizontal piece at the top of a wall or building.

Cupola: A small, decorative structure on top of the roof of a building.

Design-Bid-Build: A method of project delivery in which the architect completes construction documents and sends them out to multiple general contractors, who submit sealed bids for the job.

Design-Build: A method of project delivery in which architectural services and construction of the project are both provided through a single-source provider.

Engineering: A profession that uses technical, scientific, and mathematical knowledge to design certain aspects of a building project. Examples include:

Mechanical: Design of heat, ventilation, and air-conditioning systems (HVAC).

Plumbing: Primarily design of the hot and cold fresh-water and sewage piping for a building.

Structural: Design of the sizing and configuration of key building elements to make a structure that will withstand the forces of gravity and other forces such as wind and earthquakes.

Electrical: Design of the power and lighting systems in a building or another project.

Civil: Design of site elements such as topography, storm-water management, paving, curbs, gutters, and so forth.

Acoustical: The application of acoustical science in the design of a space or building to accomplish desired qualities of sound.

Environmental: The application of data to design for the desired level of impact on the natural environment of a site and the surrounding area. Considerations may include endangered plant and animal species and water-quality issues.

Finishes: Product coatings or materials that make a building's visual impact. Examples are paint, carpet, ceiling tile, and wood stain.

General Contractor: A company or individual in overall control of the construction process. There may be several subcontractors whom the contractor employs to work under this agreement to accomplish the work, but the general contractor is usually the only party to contract with the church for construction.

LEED (LEADERSHIP IN ENERGY AND ENVIRONMENTAL DESIGN) CERTIFICATION: One of several levels of achievement given by the Green Building Council indicating the use of certain environmentally friendly construction materials and methods. Points are accumulated for the use of design elements that achieve certain benchmarks of sustainable construction practice or performance. The project may achieve a rating from certified to platinum.

MASTER PLAN: A comprehensive plan for the physical growth of the church facilities to the saturation of the available property.

NARTHEX: The vestibule or foyer linking the main worship area, or nave, with the main entrance of a gothic-style church building or cathedral.

NAVE: Main seating area of a gothic-style rectangular church building or cathedral, usually lined with columns, where most of the congregation sits.

NEGOTIATED CONTRACT: A project-delivery method in which the contractor and the architect are both hired directly and independently by the project owner during the design process and the contract amount for construction is adjusted and negotiated as the design process continues. Generally used as a method of ensuring that a project stays within budget when the owner desires a high level of control over the quality of the construction.

PORTICO: An area outside a building that is lined with columns and covered by a roof structure.

PORTE-COCHERE (COVERED ARRIVAL AREA): A roofed area designed for vehicles to drive under for protection from the elements as they load and unload passengers.

PUNCH LIST: A list of all items remaining to be completed on a project, usually compiled at the substantial completion (90 percent) stage of construction.

RELEASE OF LIEN: A legal document, usually notarized, stating that a potential claimant will not file a lien on a property, usually indicating that all appropriate payment has been received.

REQUEST FOR PAYMENT (PAY REQUEST): A document submitted by a contractor certifying that certain tasks have been completed and materials have been purchased and stored securely and requesting that the owner pay the contracted amount.

Retainage: A portion of the payment due to the contractor, usually 5 to 10 percent, held by the church until after construction is completed.

Sacristy: A storage room for utensils and elements to be used in sacramental rites in a liturgical church building or cathedral or the utensils and elements for the ordinance of the Lord's Supper.

Schedule of Values: A breakdown of the value of each part of construction work. These figures will be the basis for the owner and the architect to review requests for payment as each part of the job is completed.

Shop Drawings: Supplemental drawings provided by a manufacturer or fabricator for manufacturing a building element or elements.

Soft Costs: Additional items besides the building construction. These costs may include site preparation, paving for parking, furnishings, audiovisual systems, equipment, architectural and engineering design fees, materials testing during construction, extending utilities to the site, zoning and building-permit fees, impact fees, and a contingency amount for miscellaneous items.

Specifications: A textural description defining the quality and standards for the major elements and workmanship that go into a building project.

Subcontractor: A person or entity working for a general contractor to provide construction services of a certain part of a project, such as concrete or steel.

Submittals: Samples of various building materials such as brick, carpet, glass, and so on, delivered for the purpose of gaining approval prior to being ordered or installed.

Substantial Completion: The point in a building project when approximately 90 percent of the work is complete and the owner can take occupancy.

Superintendent: A contractor's representative at a project site who gives day-to-day guidance to the overall construction process.

Value Engineering: The process of making and evaluating recommendations for increasing the economic efficiency of a project.

Vestry: An area designated to store robes, shawls, and other garments worn in a liturgical church or cathedral.

Zoning: The designation by a governing authority of the permissible use of a piece of property. Residential, multifamily, commercial, and industrial are examples of zoning designations. Churches are often allowed in any zoning area but may require a special-use permit to build in a certain zone.

Scriptures for Project Leaders

The following Scriptures can guide you to find and do God's will as you move through the process of planning and building a facility to serve your church. You may want to use these verses as a source for Bible study with your team, as theme Scriptures for different phases of the project, or simply as personal inspiration.

PLANNING

"You are to set up the tabernacle according to the plan for it that you have been shown on the mountain."
—Exodus 26:30

"Notice I have taken great pains to provide for the house of the Lord—3,775 tons of gold, 37,750 tons of silver, and bronze and iron that can't be weighed because there is so much of it. I have also provided timber and stone, but you will need to add more to them. You also have many workers: stonecutters, masons, carpenters, and people skilled in every kind of work in gold, silver, bronze, and iron—beyond number. Now begin the work, and may the Lord be with you."
—1 Chronicles 22:14-16

"Plans fail when there is no counsel, but with many advisers they succeed."—Proverbs 15:22

" 'I know the plans I have for you'—this is the Lord's declaration—'plans for your welfare, not for disaster, to give you a future and a hope.' "—Jeremiah 29:11

"Whoever does not bear his own cross and come after Me cannot be My disciple. For which of you, wanting to build a tower, doesn't first sit down and calculate the cost to see if he has enough to complete it? Otherwise, after he has laid the foundation and cannot finish it, all the onlookers will begin to make fun of him, saying, 'This man started to build and wasn't able to finish.' "
—Luke 14:27-30

"Everything must be done decently and in order"
—1 Corinthians 14:40

DECISION MAKING AND LEADERSHIP

"As for me, I vow that I will not sin against the Lord by ceasing to pray for you. I will teach you the good and right way."—1 Samuel 12:23

"The eyes of the Lord range throughout the earth to show Himself strong for those whose hearts are completely His."—2 Chronicles 16:9

"How happy is the man
  who does not follow the advice of the wicked,
  or take the path of sinners,
  or join a group of mockers!
  Instead, his delight is in the LORD's instruction,
  and he meditates on it day and night.
  He is like a tree planted beside streams of water
  that bears its fruit in season
  and whose leaf does not wither.
  Whatever he does prospers."—PSALM 1:1-3

"Unless the LORD builds a house,
  its builders labor over it in vain;
  unless the LORD watches over a city,
  the watchman stays alert in vain."—PSALM 127:1

"Trust in the LORD with all your heart,
  and do not rely on your own understanding;
  think about Him in all your ways,
  and He will guide you on the right paths.
  Don't consider yourself to be wise;
  fear the LORD and turn away from evil."
—PROVERBS 3:5-7

"Happy is a man who finds wisdom
  and who acquires understanding."—PROVERBS 3:13

"The reflections of the heart belong to man,
  but the answer of the tongue is from the LORD.
  All a man's ways seem right in his own eyes,

but the LORD weighs the motives.
  Commit your activities to the LORD
  and your plans will be achieved.
  A man's heart plans his way,
  but the LORD determines his steps."
—PROVERBS 16:1-3,9

"The one who pursues righteousness and faithful love
  will find life, righteousness, and honor.
  The wise conquer a city of warriors
  and bring down its mighty fortress.
  The one who guards his mouth and tongue
  keeps himself out of trouble.
  The proud and arrogant person, named 'Mocker,'
  acts with excessive pride.
  A slacker's craving will kill him
  because his hands refuse to work.
  He is filled with craving all day long,
  but the righteous give and don't hold back.
  The sacrifice of a wicked person is detestable—
  how much more so
  when he brings it with ulterior motives!"
—PROVERBS 21:21-27

"There is an occasion for everything,
  and a time for every activity under heaven:
  a time to give birth and a time to die;
  a time to plant and a time to uproot;
  a time to kill and a time to heal;
  a time to tear down and a time to build;

a time to weep and a time to laugh;
a time to mourn and a time to dance;
a time to throw stones and a time to gather stones;
a time to embrace and a time to avoid embracing;
a time to search and a time to count as lost;
a time to keep and a time to throw away;
a time to tear and a time to sew;
a time to be silent and a time to speak;
a time to love and a time to hate;
a time for war and a time for peace."
—Ecclesiastes 3:1-8

"Do not remember the past events,
pay no attention to things of old.
Look, I am about to do something new;
even now it is coming. Do you not see it?
Indeed, I will make a way in the wilderness,
rivers in the desert."—Isaiah 43:18-19

" 'You will call to Me and come and pray to Me, and I
will listen to you. You will seek Me and find Me when
you search for Me with all your heart. I will be found
by you'—the Lord's declaration—'and I will restore
your fortunes and gather you from all the nations and
places where I banished you'—the Lord's declaration.
'I will restore you to the place I deported you from.' "
—Jeremiah 29:12-14

"Whoever is faithful in very little is also faithful in
much, and whoever is unrighteous in very little is
also unrighteous in much."—Luke 16:10

"Two men went up to the temple complex to pray, one
a Pharisee and the other a tax collector. The Pharisee
took his stand and was praying like this: 'God, I thank
You that I'm not like other people—greedy, unrighteous, adulterers, or even like this tax collector. I fast
twice a week; I give a tenth of everything I get.' But the
tax collector, standing far off, would not even raise his
eyes to heaven but kept striking his chest mourning
and saying, 'God, turn Your wrath from me—a sinner!'
I tell you, this one went down to his house justified
rather than the other; because everyone who exalts
himself will be humbled, but the one who humbles
himself will be exalted."
—Luke 18:10-14

"Be strengthened by the Lord and by His vast strength.
Put on the full armor of God so that you can stand
against the tactics of the Devil. For our battle is not
against flesh and blood, but against the rulers, against
the authorities, against the world powers of this darkness, against the spiritual forces of evil in the heavens.
This is why you must take up the full armor of God,
so that you may be able to resist in the evil day, and
having prepared everything, to take your stand."
—Ephesians 6:10-13

"I am able to do all things through Him who strengthens me."—Philippians 4:13

"… keeping our eyes on Jesus, the source and perfecter of our faith, who for the joy that lay before Him endured a cross and despised the shame, and has sat down at the right hand of God's throne."
—Hebrews 12:2

"If any of you lacks wisdom, he should ask God, who gives to all generously and without criticizing, and it will be given to him."—James 1:5

"Submit to God. But resist the Devil, and he will flee from you."—James 4:7

THE TABERNACLE AND TEMPLE

"They are to make a sanctuary for Me so that I may dwell among them. You must make it according to all that I show you—the design of the tabernacle as well as the design of all its furnishings."—Exodus 25:8-9

"The temple's construction used finished stones cut at the quarry so that no hammer, chisel, or any iron tool was heard in the temple while it was being built."
—1 Kings 6:7

"My son, may the Lord be with you, and may you succeed in building the house of the Lord your God, as He said about you."—1 Chronicles 22:11

"The leaders of the households, the leaders of the tribes of Israel, the commanders of thousands and of hundreds, and the officials in charge of the king's work gave willingly. For the service of God's house they gave 185 tons of gold and 10,000 gold drachmas, 375 tons of silver, 675 tons of bronze, and 4,000 tons of iron. Whoever had precious stones gave them to the treasury of the Lord's house under the care of Jehiel the Gershonite. Then the people rejoiced because of their leaders' willingness to give, for they had given to the Lord with a whole heart. King David also rejoiced greatly."—1 Chronicles 29:6-9

"They sang with praise and thanksgiving to the Lord: 'For He is good; His faithful love to Israel endures forever.' Then all the people gave a great shout of praise to the Lord because the foundation of the Lord's house had been laid."—Ezra 3:11

"I have asked one thing from the Lord;
it is what I desire:
to dwell in the house of the Lord
all the days of my life,
gazing on the beauty of the Lord
and seeking Him in His temple.
For He will conceal me in His shelter
in the day of adversity;
He will hide me under the cover of His tent;
He will set me high on a rock.
Then my head will be high
above my enemies around me;

I will offer sacrifices in His tent with shouts of joy.
I will sing and make music to the LORD."
—PSALM 27:4-6

"I rejoiced with those who said to me,
'Let us go to the house of the LORD.' "—PSALM 122:1

"My house will be called a house of prayer
for all nations."—ISAIAH 56:7

"Very early in the morning, while it was still dark, He
got up, went out, and made His way to a deserted place.
And He was praying there."—MARK 1:35

"He told this parable: 'A man had a fig tree that was
planted in his vineyard. He came looking for fruit on it
and found none. He told the vineyard worker, "Listen,
for three years I have come looking for fruit on this fig
tree and haven't found any. Cut it down! Why should it
even waste the soil?" But he replied to him, "Sir, leave
it this year also, until I dig around it and fertilize it.
Perhaps it will bear fruit next year, but if not, you can
cut it down." ' "—LUKE 13:6-9

"In the temple complex He found people selling oxen,
sheep, and doves, and He also found the money
changers sitting there. After making a whip out of
cords, He drove everyone out of the temple complex
with their sheep and oxen. He also poured out the
money changers' coins and overturned the tables.

He told those who were selling doves, 'Get these things
out of here! Stop turning My Father's house into a
marketplace!' And His disciples remembered that
it is written: Zeal for Your house will consume Me."
—JOHN 2:14-17

"While He was in Jerusalem at the Passover Festival,
many trusted in His name when they saw the signs He
was doing. Jesus, however, would not entrust Himself
to them, since He knew them all and because He did
not need anyone to testify about man; for He Himself
knew what was in man."—JOHN 2:23-25

"The Most High does not dwell in sanctuaries
made with hands, as the prophet says:
Heaven is My throne,
and earth My footstool.
What sort of house will you build for Me?
says the Lord,
or what is My resting place?
Did not My hand make all these things?"
—ACTS 7:48-50

STEWARDSHIP, MONEY, AND POSSESSIONS

"Araunah said, 'Why has my lord the king come to his
servant?' David replied, 'To buy the threshing floor
from you in order to build an altar to the LORD, so the
plague on the people may be halted.' Araunah said to
David, 'My lord the king may take whatever he wants

and offer it. Here are the oxen for a burnt offering and the threshing sledges and ox yokes for the wood. My king, Araunah gives everything here to the king.' Then he said to the king, 'May the LORD your God accept you.' The king answered Araunah, 'No, I insist on buying it from you for a price, for I will not offer to the LORD my God burnt offerings that cost me nothing.' "
—2 SAMUEL 24:21-24

"Honor the LORD with your possessions
and with the first produce of your entire harvest;
then your barns will be completely filled,
and your vats will overflow with new wine."
—PROVERBS 3:9-10

"This is why I tell you: Don't worry about your life, what you will eat or what you will drink; or about your body, what you will wear. Isn't life more than food and the body more than clothing? Look at the birds of the sky: they don't sow or reap or gather into barns, yet your heavenly Father feeds them. Aren't you worth more than they? Can any of you add a single cubit to his height by worrying? And why do you worry about clothes? Learn how the wildflowers of the field grow: they don't labor or spin thread. Yet I tell you that not even Solomon in all his splendor was adorned like one of these! If that's how God clothes the grass of the field, which is here today and thrown into the furnace tomorrow, won't He do much more for you—you of little faith? So don't worry, saying, 'What will we eat?'

or 'What will we drink?' or 'What will we wear?' For the idolaters eagerly seek all these things, and your heavenly Father knows that you need them. But seek first the kingdom of God and His righteousness, and all these things will be provided for you. Therefore don't worry about tomorrow, because tomorrow will worry about itself. Each day has enough trouble of its own."—MATTHEW 6:25-34

"The kingdom of God is not eating and drinking, but righteousness, peace, and joy in the Holy Spirit."
—ROMANS 14:17

"It is expected of managers that each one be found faithful."—1 CORINTHIANS 4:2

"My brothers, hold your faith in our glorious Lord Jesus Christ without showing favoritism. For suppose a man comes into your meeting wearing a gold ring, dressed in fine clothes, and a poor man dressed in dirty clothes also comes in. If you look with favor on the man wearing the fine clothes so that you say, 'Sit here in a good place,' and yet you say to the poor man, 'Stand over there,' or, 'Sit here on the floor by my footstool,' haven't you discriminated among yourselves and become judges with evil thoughts?"—JAMES 2:1-4

"Based on the gift they have received, everyone should use it to serve others, as good managers of the varied grace of God."—1 PETER 4:10

"This is the confidence we have before Him: whenever we ask anything according to His will, He hears us. And if we know that He hears whatever we ask, we know that we have what we have asked Him for."
—1 John 5:14-15

BUILDING EXAMPLES

"They said to each other, 'Come, let us make oven-fired bricks.' They had brick for stone and asphalt for mortar. And they said, 'Come, let us build ourselves a city and a tower with its top in the sky. Let us make a name for ourselves; otherwise, we will be scattered over the face of the whole earth.' "—Genesis 11:3-4

"If the ax is dull, and one does not sharpen its edge, then one must exert more strength; however, the advantage of wisdom is that it brings success."—Ecclesiastes 10:10

"Because of laziness the roof caves in, and because of negligent hands the house leaks."
—Ecclesiastes 10:18

"The Lord God said:
'Look, I have laid a stone in Zion, a tested stone, a precious cornerstone, a sure foundation; the one who believes will be unshakable.' "
—Isaiah 28:16

"He showed me this: The Lord was standing there by a vertical wall with a plumb line in His hand. The Lord asked me, 'What do you see, Amos?' I replied, 'A plumb line.' Then the Lord said, 'I am setting a plumb line among My people Israel; I will no longer spare them.' "—Amos 7:7-8

"You are the light of the world. A city situated on a hill cannot be hidden. No one lights a lamp and puts it under a basket, but rather on a lampstand, and it gives light for all who are in the house. In the same way, let your light shine before men, so that they may see your good works and give glory to your Father in heaven."
—Matthew 5:14-16

"Everyone who hears these words of Mine and acts on them will be like a sensible man who built his house on the rock. The rain fell, the rivers rose, and the winds blew and pounded that house. Yet it didn't collapse, because its foundation was on the rock. But everyone who hears these words of Mine and doesn't act on them will be like a foolish man who built his house on the sand. The rain fell, the rivers rose, the winds blew and pounded that house, and it collapsed. And its collapse was great!"—Matthew 7:24-27

"When He entered Capernaum again after some days, it was reported that He was at home. So many people gathered together that there was no more room, not even in the doorway, and He was speaking the

message to them. Then they came to Him bringing a paralytic, carried by four men. Since they were not able to bring him to Jesus because of the crowd, they removed the roof above where He was. And when they had broken through, they lowered the stretcher on which the paralytic was lying. Seeing their faith, Jesus told the paralytic, 'Son, your sins are forgiven.' "
—MARK 2:1-5

"They came to Jerusalem, and He went into the temple complex and began to throw out those buying and selling in the temple. He overturned the money changers' tables and the chairs of those selling doves, and would not permit anyone to carry goods through the temple complex. Then He began to teach them: 'Is it not written, My house will be called a house of prayer for all nations? But you have made it a den of thieves!' "
—MARK 11:15-17

"On the first day of the week, we assembled to break bread. Paul spoke to them, and since he was about to depart the next day, he extended his message until midnight. There were many lamps in the room upstairs where we were assembled, and a young man named Eutychus was sitting on a window sill and sank into a deep sleep as Paul kept on speaking. When he was overcome by sleep he fell down from the third story, and was picked up dead. But Paul went down, threw himself on him, embraced him, and said, 'Don't be alarmed, for his life is in him!' "—ACTS 20:7-10

"You are God's field, God's building. According to God's grace that was given to me, as a skilled master builder I have laid a foundation, and another builds on it. But each one must be careful how he builds on it, because no one can lay any other foundation than what has been laid—that is, Jesus Christ. If anyone builds on the foundation with gold, silver, costly stones, wood, hay, or straw, each one's work will become obvious, for the day will disclose it, because it will be revealed by fire; the fire will test the quality of each one's work. If anyone's work that he has built survives, he will receive a reward. If anyone's work is burned up, it will be lost, but he will be saved; yet it will be like an escape through fire. Don't you know that you are God's sanctuary and that the Spirit of God lives in you? If anyone ruins God's sanctuary, God will ruin him; for God's sanctuary is holy, and that is what you are."
—1 Corinthians 3:9-17

"You are no longer foreigners and strangers, but fellow citizens with the saints, and members of God's household, built on the foundation of the apostles and prophets, with Christ Jesus Himself as the cornerstone. The whole building is being fitted together in Him and is growing into a holy sanctuary in the Lord, in whom you also are being built together for God's dwelling in the Spirit."—Ephesians 2:19-22

"Every house is built by someone, but the One who built everything is God."—Hebrews 3:4

"Rid yourselves of all wickedness, all deceit, hypocrisy, envy, and all slander. Like newborn infants, desire the unadulterated spiritual milk, so that you may grow by it in your salvation, since you have tasted that the Lord is good. Coming to Him, a living stone—rejected by men but chosen and valuable to God—you yourselves, as living stones, are being built into a spiritual house for a holy priesthood to offer spiritual sacrifices acceptable to God through Jesus Christ."
—1 Peter 2:1-5

"The honor is for you who believe;
but for the unbelieving,
The stone that the builders rejected—
this One has become the cornerstone, and
A stone that causes men to stumble,
and a rock that trips them up."—1 Peter 2:7-8

Construction-Project Responsibility Guide

The following guide will help churches anticipate who will accomplish each task in the planning and building process. This guide is not a comprehensive list of responsibilities for a particular project or the arrangements of any agreement. Each project is unique and may have special requirements. Agreements vary, and each project may involve a wide variety of conditions and requirements. Therefore, you should refer to your contract documents for clarification.

Most construction projects consist of three primary entities: the owner, the architect, and the contractor. There are multiple secondary roles. This guide will discuss the responsibilities of the primary roles and refer to the others who relate to these in a typical church project. Like a link in a chain, each role is important to the success of a project. A better understanding of these roles will help your church avoid problems and misunderstandings along the way.

Owner's Responsibilities
GENERAL

The owner's responsibility is to secure and pay for any and all work required for the project that is not specifically assigned to another entity in a written agreement. When the church is working with outside consultants to do various parts of the work, it is very important that the church have the consultant provide information to and cooper-ate with the architect in a timely manner so that he can coordinate the building design with this other work. Your architect can usually assist you in locating any consulting services needed for the project.

SPOKESMAN

Designate and clearly communicate to the architect, contractor, and consultants the name of your representative (and an alternate for emergencies) who has the authority to legally bind the owner to speak on behalf of the church.

LAND ACQUISITIONS/ORDINANCES

Any work required to secure property or rights is the responsibility of the owner. A real-estate professional is often enlisted to assist with this requirement.

ZONING HEARINGS

The owner must be sure that the proposed use of the project site complies with zoning laws having jurisdiction. A civil engineer usually takes the lead in this process. The architect's drawings may be required to illustrate the proposed use to gain approval. If supplemental drawings are requested, if applications need to be completed on behalf of the church, or if personal representation is required at hearings by the architect or an engineer, fees will generally be incurred for these additional services.

SITE SURVEY

At the outset of the design process, an accurate property survey is necessary. Your architect can help you obtain the required survey on request, but the church usually needs to pay for the work of the surveyor and request that the information be sent to the architect for use in designing the project.

CIVIL ENGINEERING

This professional provides the site design, including a drainage plan, site lighting, and utilities. You can select a familiar firm and direct it to work with your architect so that they can coordinate their work, or your architect may recommend a firm. Civil design is becoming increasingly more complex and highly regulated, especially in urban areas. As a result, design costs for civil engineering can be significant. The services of a civil engineer who is familiar with the local requirements are extremely helpful.

ENVIRONMENTAL ENGINEERING

Wetlands, watersheds, aquifer-recharge zones, endangered species of plants and animals, and other sensitive conditions should be thoroughly analyzed and dealt with in an appropriate manner as guided by a qualified professional. To avoid unintended environmental impact, the engineer should coordinate this work with your architect.

SOIL BORINGS

This test is required to determine the subterranean conditions that dictate the foundation design and help predict earthwork cost. The bank often requires this surface exploration when it evaluates a loan. Your architect will help you secure a geotechnical engineer and will give instructions for the necessary testing.

LEGAL COUNSEL

Before signing any agreement, the owner should seek legal advice to analyze and fully understand the terms. Legal representation may also be appropriate at other times.

INSURANCE

The owner is to purchase and maintain liability and property insurance. You are usually required to notify your insurance carrier that you are undertaking a construction project so that adjustments to coverage and premiums can be made if needed. Builder's risk insurance must be provided in the amount of the project cost but may be purchased by either the owner or the contractor, whoever can get it at the best rate.

FUND-RAISING

LifeWay Capital Stewardship has vast experience and skills in fund-raising and offers a number of campaigns, such as Together We Build®, Bridge to Tomorrow®, and Beyond Measure™. Consultants can help the church conduct fund-raising activities, and services are available on a fee basis. Because a successful campaign can significantly increase the funds available for the project or reduce the amount that has to be borrowed, it can have a major impact on your project. Call (800) 251-4220 for information.

FINANCING

Most of the time the church will need to work with lending institutions to negotiate and secure loans for interim construction financing. The owner must also arrange permanent financing, including closing costs. If requested, you may be required to provide your contractor reasonable evidence that financial arrangements have been made. Southern Baptist churches can call on the North American Mission Board (*www.churchfinanceministry.com*) for loans, assistance in preparing a financial statement, and finding a lender.

ACOUSTICAL CONSULTANT

Projects that involve critical sound considerations call for the skills of a professional acoustical consultant. Your architect will help the church employ a professional to provide these services and will coordinate this work with the building-design team.

SOUND REINFORCEMENT AND VIDEO CONSULTANT(S)

The design of sound reinforcement and video-projection systems is a specialty that is normally involved in worship-facility design and other similar projects. This design is a separate function from designing the acoustics of the room; however, some acoustical engineers also design sound and video systems. These services can be offered as design-build, with the designer also installing the system. Some churches prefer to have a system designed by a professional then bid to various companies for the installation.

THEATRICAL LIGHTING

Some areas of the church facility may require theatrical lighting. The same company that provides sound equipment may install the lighting but not necessarily. Your architect will coordinate the design with your consultant and the electrical engineer to accommodate this design element.

SECURITY SYSTEM

Usually, the owner directly handles both the design and the installation of the security system. Be sure your alarm company cooperates with your architect, who will also coordinate with the electrical engineer for location and power requirements.

LANDSCAPING

In some cases the city requires the church to have a professional landscape designer select species and design the layout of plantings and an irrigation system for the property. Your architect will coordinate this work with that of the civil engineer.

SIGNAGE

Design of site signage, building signs, interior way-finding signage, and room labels are not usually provided under the architectural contract. Your architect may be willing to assist you but may require an additional fee to do so, or you may wish to work directly with a specialist in this field.

KITCHEN CONSULTANT

Your architect can recommend a specialist in this field to design and specify equipment. Some kitchen-consulting firms provide this service as design-build, with the designer also selling you the equipment; others create specifications so that the equipment can be competitively bid. This work needs to be coordinated through the architect and the various engineering disciplines to ensure proper connections for the equipment.

INTERIOR DESIGN/COLOR SELECTIONS

Finish and special color selections are the responsibility of the church. Your architect can assist you in employing a designer to provide interior design services that will select wall colors, carpet, flooring, floor patterns, wood stain, ceiling tiles, fabric for pews, grille cloth, curtains, lighting and plumbing fixtures and trim, and so forth. The architect's basic services will include routine room finishes and fixture selection.

TELEPHONE/COMMUNICATIONS/ COMPUTERS

Your architect will usually coordinate this work with the designer of your systems.

FURNISHINGS

Usually, the church directly selects and contracts all furniture, broadly defined as any item that is not attached to the building. This normally includes pews, although your architect can advise and assist in this selection. Manufacturer's representatives will make presentations to the church to help you decide whose products you want to use. The church should budget for and select other furniture. Selecting furniture may or may not be a part of the services of your interior designer. Your architect can put you in touch with a consultant to assist in this task.

REIMBURSABLE EXPENSES

The church will pay for site-visit travel expenses; long-distance services; printings and reproductions of the drawings and project documents required for the design and construction process; postage, handling, and delivery; any overtime work authorized by the owner; and renderings, models, professional photography, and presentation material requested by the owner. These expenses can be a substantial expense that should be included in the project budget.

PRICING/BUDGET ESTIMATION

The church is strongly urged to seek the assistance of a professional estimator or contractor to evaluate the project and make cost projections to determine whether the cost is within the available funds. This estimate should be done early in the process to minimize the risk and extent of fees for redesign that can be required by your architect and engineers. Your architect may be willing to assist with the interview and selection of a qualified estimator on request.

VALUE ENGINEERING

Once pricing has been done, the church may want to explore options for reducing the cost of the project, known as value engineering. The estimator or an independent entity can provide this service. Many general contractors offer estimating and value engineering at little or no cost for the opportunity to be involved in your project early in the process. Be sure they give this phase of the work the attention it deserves, or some nasty surprises can result.

SELECTING CONTRACTORS

After the construction documents are complete and bids are received, the owner needs to evaluate and select the contractor who will carry out the construction. Your architect will usually participate in the evaluation of bids and will assist in the selection process.

AGREEMENTS WITH CONTRACTORS

The church needs to negotiate a contract for construction with the contractor. Your architect should assist you in evaluating the terms of the contract, but legal services are usually required as well.

TESTING

As the construction proceeds, the specifications usually require materials and construction work to be tested for quality-control purposes. Many of these tests are items the building code calls special inspections. Some tests may be included in the general contractor's agreement; others are the responsibility of the owner. These tests will be arranged by the contractor and accomplished by an independent testing lab. The results will be provided to the architect and the owner. Payment for testing services will be the responsibility of the owner. Sometimes the tests reveal structural conditions or materials that need to be tested for the presence of hazardous materials. The owner is required to pay for the process of investigation and for obtaining samples and sending them to a qualified laboratory.

REVIEWING SUBMITTALS

When the owner needs to approve or select materials and colors, samples will be made available to the church for review. Your architect will make a recommendation for a selection, approval, or rejection in a timely manner. Items that require decisions include brick, glass, flooring, base, paint colors, roofing materials, and so on.

APPROVING PAY REQUESTS

The contractor should submit requests for payment to your architect. The architect will review these and recommend that the church pay, adjust, or reject these requests. The church is responsible for taking action and making sure bills are paid in a timely manner according to the terms of the agreement with the contractor.

KEYING OF DOORS

The church needs to work with the hardware subcontractor to coordinate the keying of doors so that new buildings can be keyed to integrate into a master key system or as you require.

STOP-WORK ORDER

It is the church's responsibility to issue a written order to stop work if the contractor persistently fails to carry out work in accordance with the contract documents (plans and specifications). Your architect may recommend this action. This order will maintain certain owner rights under the typical contract. See your construction contract and secure the services of a lawyer for details and guidance if necessary.

PAYING THE ARCHITECT, CONTRACTOR, AND CONSULTANTS

The church should have funds available to pay invoices in a timely manner, usually defined as 30 or fewer days.

Architect's Responsibilities
ARCHITECTURAL DRAWINGS

Your architect will provide drawings to show the desired configuration of the building and to provide information to the church, contractor, engineers, and government regulators about the desired outcome of the building project.

MECHANICAL ENGINEERING

The architect will employ and coordinate the work of a licensed professional to design a system of heat, ventilation, and air conditioning for the building according to the applicable codes.

PLUMBING ENGINEERING

The architect will employ and coordinate the work of a licensed professional to design a system of domestic hot and cold water, sewerage, and selection of fixtures according to the current applicable codes.

ELECTRICAL ENGINEERING

The architect will employ and coordinate the work of a licensed professional to design a system of electrical power and lighting for the interior and exterior. This may or may not include site lighting. This work will be coordinated with the civil engineer's service.

STRUCTURAL ENGINEERING

The architect will employ and coordinate with the work of a licensed professional to design the structural system and its elements, using current building-code standards as a minimum requirement. The structure normally includes foundation design, roof and floor framing, roof- and floor-load calculations, and earthquake or hurricane loading requirements. It also includes support for special structures such as a steeple, a sign, or other elements that are part of the building.

BUILDING-CODE RESEARCH

The architect should design the building to meet or exceed the minimum standards set by the current edition of the applicable codes, as adopted and amended by your local jurisdiction. Codes typically address ways to make facilities for public assembly structurally sound, adequately ventilated, fire safe, accessible to the disabled, and provided with adequate exits. The architect will work with building officials to achieve approvals both before and during the permitting process.

COORDINATING ALL MAJOR DISCIPLINES

By incorporating the work of various professionals in the design of the building, the architect attempts to avoid conflicts in the various elements of construction. When conflicts arise, your architect will work to resolve them in a way that achieves the intent of the designs, satisfies pertinent code requirements, and meets the needs of the owner.

ARCHITECTURAL SPECIFICATIONS

Your architect will provide this extensive textural description to define the quality and standards for each of the major elements and workmanship that go into the project.

OBSERVING CONSTRUCTION

Your architect, the consulting engineers, and/or their representatives will visit the site and/or examine photographic evidence throughout the construction project to inspect the work as it progresses. Because the architect cannot be there at all times, he cannot guarantee that the contractor's work complies with the drawings; but he will look for any problems that occur in the process of construction. When necessary, the architect will recommend that the church reject work that is not in compliance with the construction documents. He will require that it be corrected before payment is authorized for that portion of the work and will convey this information to the contractor.

REVIEWING SHOP DRAWINGS

The various subcontractors on the project submit detailed supplemental drawings. Your architect and the engineers will review these drawings for general compliance with the design intent and will approve or reject them. Building elements that are to be fabricated for the project, such as structural steel, cabinetry, toilet partitions, precast elements, and millwork, are usually included

REVIEWING SUBMITTALS

The architect will review submittals of samples and materials as called for in the specifications. When the owner's approval or selection is called for, samples will be made available to the church for review as well. Your architect will make a recommendation for selection, approval, or rejection in a timely manner. Items that require decisions include brick, glass, flooring, base, paint colors, roofing materials, and so on.

REVIEWING PAY REQUESTS

Your architect will review requests for payment, usually submitted monthly by the contractor along with releases of liens, if required. The architect will recommend that the church pay, adjust, or reject each request.

Contractor's Responsibilities
BUDGET AND COST ANALYSIS

It is the task of the contractor or a professional estimator to estimate the cost to construct the project, including all pertinent permits, fees, labor, and materials necessary to complete the job, based on the architect's drawings.

VALUE-ENGINEERING ANALYSIS

In some cases the contractor assists the owner and the architect by making recommendations for increasing the project's economic efficiency. This service may require the owner to provide additional compensation.

PERMITS AND FEES

The contractor generally applies for the appropriate permits required to undertake the project on behalf of the church. In some cases application fees and others, such as impact fees, are a part of this process. The church should verify which fees have been accounted for in the contractor's bid for construction and which will be the direct responsibility of the church.

CONSTRUCTION SCHEDULE

The contractor is to provide a schedule and sequence of the work to ensure a smooth flow according to the terms agreed on in the owner-contractor agreement. Contractors need to be made aware if the church will remain in operation in and around the project location. Cleanup and access to the buildings, parking, and other facilities need to be clarified in the contract for construction.

SCHEDULE OF VALUES

The contractor provides a breakdown of the value of each part of the construction work. On this basis the owner and the architect review the requests for payment as each part of the project is completed.

TAX-EXEMPT PROCESS

In some cases the church may claim tax-exempt status for the purchase of the materials for the building. If this exemption applies in your state, ask the contractor to help you obtain this savings. This procedure also needs to be included in the contract for construction.

UTILITY COORDINATION

The contractor works with the utility companies to tie in to their services and to arrange with the church when service will be interrupted.

REVIEWING SHOP DRAWINGS

Before submitting shop drawings to the architect for approval, the contractor reviews them for compliance with the contract documents.

REVIEWING SUBMITTALS

The contractor submits samples of materials to the architect for approval, such as brick, glass, flooring, base, paint colors, roofing materials, and so on, as called for in the specifications.

CONSTRUCTION

It is the task of the contractor to build the project. The contractor provides guidance to the subcontractors in the methods of construction, maintaining quality workmanship and a clean, safe job site throughout construction.

SUPERINTENDENT

The contractor employs a person to be on site to guide the work and to run the project whenever work is in progress. An assistant may be designated to take over when the superintendent is not able to be there. The superintendent ensures that the project meets the schedule agreed on and the quality called for in the design documents, while maintaining a safe work environment.

PAY REQUESTS

The contractor assembles progress statements from the subcontractors and reviews these before submitting them to the architect for approval. The contractor prepares monthly pay requests using industry-standard forms for submittal to the architect and the owner. Pay requests will refer to the schedule of values and will indicate what portion of the work has been completed, the amount previously paid, and how much is owed.

RELEASES OF LIEN

The contractor obtains and submits releases of lien from the subcontractors indicating that payment has been received for work accomplished. This step may be done on a monthly basis or at the end of the project and is usually dictated by the lending institution holding the construction loan for the project.

JOB CLOSEOUT

The contractor cleans the building and the site and gets the building ready for occupancy. He or his representative gives the church information about the maintenance of materials and the operation of systems in the building, providing copies of the owner's manual for the equipment and materials incorporated. He also provides written information about the guarantees or warranties for systems or products in the building.

Change Orders:
The Bad-News Bearers
of Building Projects

CHANGE ORDERS. These words have arguably created more havoc, disputes, claims, and ill feelings than any others in the design and construction industry. But the way they are handled can lessen some of your headaches when change orders are necessary.

Change orders are documents that direct a contractor to make changes in the construction of a project that affect the schedule and/or the contracted price of the project. They can arise for several reasons.

THE OWNER uses change orders to direct changes for any reason that need to be documented as part of the project because they affect the cost and/or the schedule of the contractor's work. Change orders are also needed when the owner requests changes that affect elements of the design such as occupancies, exits, or other elements that may need to be reviewed for code compliance or elements such as mechanical loads or structural features.

THE ARCHITECT uses change orders to initiate changes in order to address code or zoning compliance, constructability, or other elements necessary to complete the construction project. As a structure goes up, it may become apparent that changes are required to make the design better, more sustainable, or more serviceable. Usually, these elements would have cost about the same amount of money if anticipated in the design stage but were omitted for some reason.

CONTRACTORS use change orders to address items not originally included in the project bid or to adapt plans to coordinate or correct unforeseen items that were discovered during the progress of the work. Bad soil conditions are one of the most common sources of this type of change order. Removing rock or unsatisfactory soil and replacing it with suitable soil can be expensive. Sometimes one error can necessitate other changes to accommodate or compensate for the error. These may or may not affect the cost of the building, but they usually affect the time of construction.

Here are some commonly asked questions and answers about change orders that can help you deal with them more effectively.

HOW AND WHEN WILL I BE INFORMED ABOUT CHANGES THAT ARISE?

After reviewing the proposed change in cost submitted by the contractor, your architect will prepare and present change orders for your review and execution and will discuss the causes or purposes of the requested changes.

WHO CAN AUTHORIZE A CHANGE ORDER?

All parties involved in a design and construction project can request that changes be made, but only the owner is empowered to approve them.

The architect has the authorization to make minor changes in the work as long as the contract sum or time is not changed.

DO ALL CHANGE ORDERS INCREASE THE COST OF THE PROJECT?

No. Although a greater percentage of change orders add to the contracted cost, some change orders can be requested that reduce the cost; however, care must be taken not to disproportionately reduce the quality or value to the owner.

HOW CAN I AVOID OR LIMIT UNDESIRABLE CHANGE ORDERS?

It is not realistic to completely eliminate change orders from a project. Focus your efforts on managing the number of change orders, budgeting time in the schedule and dollars in your budget to allow for the change orders that are needed.

You can reduce the risk of excessive change orders by following these guidelines.

COMMUNICATION. Communication among the church, the architect, and the contractor is essential to minimizing the number of change orders. Ask lots of questions to be sure what you intend is actually represented in the design documents and on the construction site.

SCHEDULE. Allow the architect adequate time to perform his services. Project schedules that are compressed during the design phase have a higher risk for change orders.

ARCHITECT SELECTION. Select a highly qualified architect to allow you to anticipate much of what is ahead for the building project. An architect may have the lowest fee because he intends to spend less time on the project. This plan can lead to changes later in the process.

CONTRACTOR SELECTION. Do a thorough reference check before signing an agreement for construction with a contractor. On large projects even major subcontractors should be reviewed before signing an agreement. The lowest bid on a project may be a result of items that were omitted from the bid. Closely examine the bids and look for large discrepancies that may indicate omissions. Even if they are unintentional omissions, they can come back to cost you in the form of a change order.

TESTING. Testing of the site and existing conditions can prevent many change orders. Core samples investigating soil conditions early in the project can discover conditions that would be unwelcome surprises later. Testing for asbestos, contaminated soils, percolation, and other environmental issues are required in some jurisdictions and might be a good idea anywhere the possibility exists. These tests will not eliminate the expense from the budget but will allow you to anticipate the actual cost of the project earlier and adjust other elements of the design to compensate if necessary.

REVIEW. Actively participate in the review of the design documents at various phases of the project. Encourage individual departments to review their specific areas and to comment in writing. Document your comments in writing to your architect and keep a copy for your records. Always date any changes requested on drawings.

CHANGE-ORDER PROCESS. Ask your architect to present the change-order process and to explain the impact changes can have on your project.

CONSTRUCTION WORK PLAN. Ask your contractor to prepare a work plan for your project. Often, complex details can be decided in advance and discrepancies can be discovered, helping your project run more smoothly and further reducing the risk of change orders.

CONSTRUCTION PROCESS. Pay close attention to the construction process. Identifying change orders early can reduce their impact on the project.

Remember to maintain a reasonable contingency fund throughout the project, from design through construction, to allow for change orders that may arise. This amount will vary from as much as 10 to 20 percent early in the project to around 2 to 5 percent after bidding and during construction.

Sample Church Inventory

XYZ CHURCH WORSHIP-CENTER INVENTORY

The planning team is gathering opinions about a proposed new worship building. This survey is not a vote but an inventory of ideas that will be considered in the planning process before a design is recommended to the church.

Age (circle one)

| 6–12 | 13–18 | 19–24 | 25–35 | 36–45 | 46–55 | 56–65 | 66–75 | 76 up |

Are you a member of XYZ Church?   Yes   No

Check the appropriate column to indicate whether you agree or disagree with each of the following statements.

	AGREE	NOT SURE	DISAGREE
The existing XYZ Church building should continue to be used for worship.			
The existing XYZ Church building should transition to other ministry use.			
I would attend Sunday-morning Bible-study classes if offered for my age group.			
I would give generously to help the church accomplish its goals.			
Other comments:			

Check the appropriate column to indicate the priority you would place on each of the following items in the new worship center.

	HIGH IMPORTANCE	MEDIUM IMPORTANCE	LOW IMPORTANCE
Large seating capacity			
Comfortable seating			
Seating close to platform			
Large platform with room for additional instruments			
Large choir loft			
High-quality audiovisual equipment			
Windows/natural light in worship center			
Windows/natural light in foyer/atrium			
Large foyer/gathering area			
Ample number of stalls in restrooms			
High-quality offices/administration area			
Nicely landscaped property and grounds			
Attractive church sign			
Ample parking			
Accessibility to the disabled			
Large, state-of-the-art nursery			
Large, state-of-the-art preschool and children's classrooms			
Weekday day-care/day-school facilities			
Ample, high-quality youth and adult classrooms			
Music-ministry rehearsal and storage space			
Media center/library			
Gym/recreation area			
Other:			

LifeWay Resources

LifeWay Christian Resources offers a wide range of fee-based services to assist churches and other ministry organizations with planning construction projects. This team of experienced and highly ministry-oriented architects and other specialists can add the benefit of their wisdom to your project. LifeWay is a nonprofit organization that does mission work and contributes to ministry efforts such as the Cooperative Program and other ministries to further the work of the church and spread the gospel of Jesus Christ around the world. Services include the following.

ON-SITE CONSULTATION. A consultant will visit your church to evaluate the existing facilities, dialogue with your planning group, and help you begin the planning process.

MASTER PLANNING. LifeWay professionals can create a comprehensive plan for the stewardship of your church property, including presentation drawings and an artist's rendering of proposed construction to serve as both important planning instruments and motivational tools in your fund-raising efforts.

ARCHITECTURAL SERVICES. In many states LifeWay's architects can provide full services for the creation of plans and specifications for bidding and permitting all the way through the construction administration. All services are offered on a fee basis as a ministry to help churches build the best facilities for their situation and to put the church in the best possible position to minister and grow. Contact us at (615) 251-2466. Many other resources are available on our Web site at *www.lifeway.com/arch*.

CAPITAL-STEWARDSHIP SERVICES. LifeWay offers a full range of high-quality stewardship resources and services to make your fund-raising effort the best it can be. Contact us at (800) 251-4220. Visit our Web site at *www.lifeway.com/cs*.

Photo Index

The following projects depicted in this book were
designed by the architects of LifeWay Architecture.

Photos on pages 170–71 are used by permission of Pastor Mark McManus;
New Hope Baptist Church; Yellville, Arkansas.